RAISEYOUTHRIGHT

The Essential Money Skills Handbook for Teens

First edition

Advisor: Richard Meadows

This book was professionally typeset on Reedsy.
Find out more at reedsy.com

Contents

VIII   Part 8 - Beyond Personal Finance

Preface

Imagine standing in a store, locked in a stare-off with the latest iPhone model or electric guitar or whatever you've been dreaming about. A question starts nagging at you: Should I buy it? No, it's not just about deciding between splurging now or saving for later – you're molding the shape of your financial destiny.

Flashback to my younger self, money was like a foreign language. How should I juggle my allowance? What's the most savvy way to save up for the OG Xbox I'd been drooling over? And, heavens, don't even get me started on those sleepless nights worrying about college fees. It seemed like every choice came with its own price tag, and I was caught in an endless tug-of-war between living in the moment and squirreling away for the 'big stuff.'

In hindsight, I wish someone had whispered in my ear that it's totally okay not to have all the answers, that money wisdom is a journey, not a birthright, and that achieving financial victory often comes down to a blend of smart spending and steady saving. But let's be real when you're a teenager, it's tough to look past the sparkle of that next best thing or the allure of the latest fashion wave.

That's why this book is here. It's your companion on this rollercoaster ride of mastering money management. Whether you feel like you've got a handle on your finances, or you're still puzzling over the difference between debit and credit, this book is loaded with the tools and insights you need to navigate the maze of money decisions with confidence. Trust me, your future self is going to high-five you!

Who Am I?

Hi, I'm Scarlett Rivers. Not too long ago, I was just like you, trying to make sense of my place in the big wide world of money. Thoughts like "how will I ever afford college?" and "how can I make my money last until the end of the month?" would keep me up at night. The pressure to manage my finances right, from my folks, my teachers, and, let's be honest, myself, felt heavier than a wallet full of coins. I was desperate to crack the code to becoming a money mastermind and finding financial stability and freedom.

Reflecting on my journey, it's clear that my financial journey was not only shaped by my decisions but also the experiences I stumbled upon, the people who shared their wisdom with me, and those oh-so-important life lessons I learned from making mistakes. The big revelation? Money management isn't about predicting the future - it's about preparing for it, whatever it might look like.

I remember being a teen, just like you, trying to navigate the complex maze of money matters. I could have really used a map – something to guide me and demystify the world of finances. So, I decided to create that guide and wrote this book. My mission? To help you understand the ins and outs of money, weigh your options, and create a personal financial plan that works for you. I want to arm you with the knowledge and tools you need to handle whatever financial curveballs life might throw your way.

Whether you're just beginning to grasp the concept of money or you've already started your journey towards financial literacy, this book is for you. Consider it your roadmap to navigating the intricacies of money management, exploring your financial potential, and building the skills you need to achieve financial success, whatever that looks like for you.

Why This Book and Why Now?

Managing money? It's a pretty big deal, especially when you're a teen. It's not just about budgeting your allowance or saving up for that new game. It's about understanding the value of money, making smart financial decisions, and finding your stride in this whirlwind world of finances. That's a heap of responsibility when you're already trying to juggle schoolwork, social life, and just growing up.

But the complexity of money management? It's just the beginning. The financial landscape is ever-evolving, more unpredictable than a chameleon in a rainbow. Digital currencies are emerging, online transactions are booming, and the concept of money we once knew is shifting. Navigating this financial maze can feel daunting, especially when you're just starting to understand it.

Let's throw in the unique hurdles of being a teen in today's world. You're living in an era of instant gratification, with online shopping and digital transactions making money seem almost invisible. You're trying to figure out your financial footing in a world where economic upheavals and global crises can shake things up without warning. And you're seeing massive global issues, like climate change and inequality, which require mindful and ethical financial choices.

Then came the pandemic, like a curveball thrown into our lives, changing the way we handle and perceive money. It's like someone tossed our financial rulebook into the air, shifting our focus to online banking, e-commerce, and the importance of emergency savings. It's been a clear signal that flexibility is crucial when dealing with unpredictable scenarios. That's why we need a clear, straight-shooting guide to help you make sense of this financial labyrinth.

I get it, I really do. I remember being a teen, with so many questions and uncertainties about money and my financial future. It was a cocktail of stress, confusion, anticipation, and, let's be real, a bit of fear. But now, armed with my experiences, lessons learned, and insights from mentoring other teens, I want to share what I've learned along the way.

And that's why this book exists. I believe that with the right knowledge and a little guidance, you can master the complex world of money management. You can learn to budget effectively, save wisely, and make informed financial decisions that align with your goals. You can face the future not with trepidation or doubt, but with confidence and a sense of preparedness.

This book is here to assist you in making smart choices about your financial future. It's about handing over the control to you to steer your own financial journey, explore your options, and build a financial roadmap that feels both fulfilling and attainable. With everything that's happening in the world right now, there's no better time to start understanding and mastering money skills.

Why Not Other Money-Related Books for Teens?

Back in my teenage years, I was on an epic mission to take control of my finances. I tore through a mountain of money-related books, hoping to unearth some wisdom that could change my life. Reflecting on that time, I see a few reasons why those books didn't quite hit the spot:

Sweeping Concepts Without Practical Tools

Some of those reads overflowed with big ideas and common advice, but they fell short when it came to practical, down-to-earth tools I could use in real life. I was looking for strategies I could apply immediately, not just grand theories that swirled around in my head without landing.

Overly Complex Language

Others hurled complicated financial terms and models at me. I mean, they seemed pretty impressive, but they were more like trying to unlock a secret code while I was still trying to figure out what money was all about. I needed something that felt more like a friendly chat, not a rocket science lecture that made my head spin.

Good Advice, Boring Presentation

Then there were the books that actually had decent advice. But if I'm honest, they were about as exciting as watching a snail crawl. I'd finish them, feel a surge of inspiration that faded faster than a popsicle in the sun, and then forget all about them by the next week. The advice didn't really stick or spark me to grab the bull by the horns when it came to my finances.

Don't get me wrong. There are some seriously amazing finance books out there that are worth every cent. But, it struck me that there was a hole that needed filling.

When I decided to pass on what I'd learned about managing money, I wanted to flip the script. No vague theories or overwhelming you with financial jargon. I wanted to give you real, hands-on strategies that helped me understand my finances. And above all, I wanted to present it in a way that's fun, easy to get, and tailored just for you – the rising generation ready to steer the ship of your financial future.

So here's the deal. This book is designed to be your trusty sidekick, penned by someone who's been in your sneakers. I'm not here to tell you how to manage your money, but to equip you with the know-how, tools, and confidence to make savvy decisions about your own financial destiny.

Navigating This Book

You're on the brink of embarking on a thrilling journey into the universe of money, with this book serving as your trusty compass. It's written in a friendly, engaging style that's all about you. And guess what? We've included quizzes at the end of each part to reinforce your learning. Get ready for a sneak peek into this exciting adventure!

Our expedition commences with 'Understanding Money', like decoding the secret language of the currency cosmos. Here, we'll dissect the significance of money, what gives it value, and its influence on today's society. We'll even touch upon the future of money, including a glimpse into digital currencies.

Next, we venture into Banks and Jobs. Here, you'll unravel the mechanics of banks and learn to harness them to your advantage. Additionally, we'll explore ways to earn money, from traditional jobs to digital-age side hustles.

In 'Budgeting, Spending, and Saving', we'll transform you into a finance-savvy wizard. You'll acquire skills to create your own budget, make smart spending decisions, and save proficiently.

'Borrowing and Credit' unfolds the good, the bad, and the ugly aspects of debt and credit scores. Brace yourself for an all-inclusive guide to understanding these complex yet essential components of grown-up life.

Although 'Planning and Financing Your Future' might seem distant, it's incredibly relevant. This section primes you for hefty expenses like college, a car, or even your first house. Plus, we'll lay the groundwork for a comfortable retirement.

In 'Investing', we'll demystify the stock market and other investment avenues. Heard the phrase "make your money work for you"? This is what they're referring to!

Next up, 'Beyond Personal Finance' propels us into the realm of philanthropy and understanding your paycheck and taxes. Here, you'll learn to be a conscious, well-informed citizen.

Finally, 'Navigating Financial Risk' is about learning to safeguard your finances. We'll examine potential traps like fraud and identity theft and how to dodge them, and delve into the basics of insurance and the importance of understanding contracts.

Just a quick note before we dive in – you don't have to binge-read this book like the newest season of your favorite Netflix show. Actually, it's way better if you don't. This book is designed to be your sidekick on your money journey, not some scary textbook you've got to cram the night before an exam.

Feel free to take it slow. Break up the reading, and maybe dive into the sections that make you think, "Hey, this is pretty cool." Let your brain soak up the information, think about it, and see how it fits into your world. And the quizzes at the end of each section? They're your own personal cheat codes to remember what you've learned.

This book is your tool. You can flip it open whenever you need a quick fact check or a deep dive into a money topic. Remember, you're the driver on this road to money mastery. We're just here riding shotgun, helping you navigate. So buckle up and enjoy the ride!

Are you prepared to plunge into this monumental money quest? Let's get started!

I

Part 1 - Understanding Money

Chapter 1 - Money 101: What's the Deal?

The Real Reason We Can't Live Without Cash

Alright, time travelers, welcome back to the present! Now that we've strolled through the history of money, let's dig into the real deal - why do we even need money?

Now, wouldn't it be cool if we could just pick up the latest gaming console or stroll into a concert without having to count our pennies? Life seems like it'd be easier without money, doesn't it? But let's game out a world without cash for a sec.

Picture this - you're a total boss at making cupcakes. Your cupcakes are the talk of the town, and everyone's lining up for them. You decide you want to trade these sweet treats for something you need, let's say, a pair of sneakers. So, you find a dude with killer sneakers, and you offer up your cupcakes. But uh-oh, he's not a fan of cupcakes. He's craving pizza.

So now, you're on a mission to find someone who has pizza and wants cupcakes. Once you've found this unicorn, you then take that pizza to the sneaker guy to finally grab your new kicks. It feels like running a marathon, doesn't it?

That's precisely the problem folks had back in the days of bartering. Trading goods directly was a royal pain. Plus, it was super tough to figure out how many cupcakes equal a pizza or a pair of sneakers.

And this, dear friends, is why money was a total game-changer. Whether you're trading for sneakers, pizza, or cupcakes, money gives it a common value. It makes the whole trading game a ton easier and way more efficient.

Just think about it. With money, you can sell your cupcakes to anyone who's interested, and they give you money in return. You then use that dough to buy anything you want - sneakers, concert tickets, and even more ingredients to bake more cupcakes.

Money is also your best bud when it comes to saving. Want a new gaming laptop? You can stash away a bit of money until you have enough. Try doing that with cupcakes!

Money's also a super tool for planning for the future. It allows us to cater to our needs and dreams, be it going to college, launching a business, or even kicking back in retirement one day.

So, money isn't just shiny coins or crisp notes or numbers on a screen. It's a system that helps us trade easier, save for what we want, and gives us the freedom to choose what we want to do with the value of our work or stuff.

The Secret Behind Why Money Is Valuable

Alright, let's take a moment to ponder this - why is a simple piece of paper, a shiny coin, or some numbers on a screen considered valuable? I mean, why can these things get you your favorite snack, the latest bestselling book, or even a slick, new bicycle? It's kind of mind-boggling if you stop and think about it.

So, here's the deal: Money is like a promise we all make to each other. We've all agreed that these pieces of paper, these bits of metal, or these digital numbers mean something. They're like golden tickets that we can swap for the stuff we want or need.

But let's take a closer look - the actual stuff that money is made from - the paper, the metal, or even the digital codes - aren't super valuable on their own. Like, you couldn't trade a regular piece of notebook paper for a delicious slice of pepperoni pizza, could you? But once that paper gets transformed into a bill, stamped by the government, and agreed upon by everyone as money - voila! Suddenly, that piece of paper holds value.

So, the million-dollar question is: where does this value come from? A long time ago, many countries used a system called the "gold standard." This system meant that for every piece of money out there - every bill or coin - the government kept a matching amount of gold in a safe place. Because gold has been seen as valuable for a long time, it seemed sensible to base money's value on it.

But, fast-forward to now, most countries have said goodbye to the gold standard. These days, the value of our money comes from the trust and faith we have in our economy and our government. When we believe our economy is rock solid and our government is doing a good job, we trust that our money is valuable. This trust lets us go out and swap that money for the goods and services we want or need.

But, here's the catch - trust can be a bit wobbly. When people start doubting the economy or the government, the value of money can start sliding downhill. Maybe you've heard about this happening in some places, where money loses its value super quickly and prices for everyday stuff just shoot up. This scary scenario is known as inflation, and we'll dig deeper into it in the next chapter.

So, in a nutshell, money has value because we all agree it does. It's a system built on trust, a promise that these pieces of paper, metal, or digital numbers can be traded for real things we want or need. It's a little weird when you really think about it, but hey, it's been working for centuries!

Keep this concept in mind as we keep exploring the world of money.

Money's Role In Today's Society

So, when you start earning money – whether from a part-time job, a full-time job, or hey, even from the best lemonade stand in town – a part of what you make goes to these things called taxes. Yeah, I know, sounds like a bummer. But wait up. These taxes are the juice that keeps our communities running. They fund all the stuff we all use and need like roads, schools, parks, and hospitals. So, when you're paying taxes, you're actually doing your bit for your community and your country. Now that's pretty cool, isn't it?

Next up – charity. Life's a rollercoaster and sometimes, folks find themselves in a tight spot. Maybe there's been a natural disaster, or they're just going through a rough patch. This is where charity steps in. People with big hearts (just like you!) can help out by donating some of their money. This cash can then be used to provide food, shelter, and medical care to those who really need a helping hand. So, money's not just a tool for getting what you want. It's also a powerful tool for helping others.

And don't forget, money can also open doors for your future! Have you been eyeing that new computer? Or dreaming about college, starting your own business, or just chilling in retirement one day? By saving and sometimes even investing our money, we can turn these dreams into reality. Think of every penny you save as a seed you're planting for your future. The more you plant, the more your future blooms!

Here's the deal – money's not all about grabbing the latest games or the coolest clothes (even though that's pretty awesome, no doubt). It's also about how we connect with each other and with the world we live in. Money is a tool we use to trade, to lend a hand, and to give back to society.

Knowing your way around money is super important. The more you get the hang of it, the better you'll be at making choices – how to earn it, how to spend it, how to save it, and even how to grow it. And that, my friend, is what being money-savvy is all about. So, high-five to you for getting this far – you're on your way to becoming a real whizz at handling money. Buckle up, because our journey's just getting started!

Chapter 2 - Understanding Currency and Inflation

Currency Demystified: Unraveling the What and the How

Currency is actually just a fancy word for money - the same dough you'd hand over for your beloved comic book or that latest video game that's got you hyped. But here's a twist, currency doesn't only live in your wallet or piggy bank, it's also living large in the digital world, like the digits in your bank account, or in mysterious things called cryptocurrencies like Bitcoin.

Let's first zoom in on the physical currencies – coins and bills. These little fellas come in a rainbow of shapes, sizes, and colors. Think of the shiny quarters and dimes hiding between your couch cushions or the fresh dollar bills chilling in your wallet. The thing about these physical forms of money is they're tangible, you can hold them, feel them, and yep, even misplace them under your bed (don't sweat it, it happens to the best of us).

Now, each country usually rolls with its own type of currency. So, the US has dollars, the UK deals with pounds, Japan in yen, and so on. Kinda like each country speaking its own money language.

Next up, let's take a peek into the future of currency - welcome to the era of digital moolah. Instead of being something you can physically feel, digital money lives entirely in the electronic realm. Picture the money in your online bank account, or those handy-dandy online gift cards. You can't physically hold them, but they'll still bag you some cool stuff, just like coins and bills.

Then there's the cryptic world of cryptocurrencies, like Bitcoin. These types of digital currencies are decentralized – which means they're not under the thumb of any government or central bank. Wild, right? But don't worry, we'll take a deeper dive into the enigma of cryptocurrencies a little later.

So, whether it's a fistful of coins, a wad of bills, or a digital code floating in cyberspace, currency is our VIP pass to trade. It's a global way of saying, "Hey, swap you this for that." It's all about the art of the deal, and it's what keeps the world's economic engine revving.

Remember, every fragment of currency, be it a humble penny or a digital Bitcoin, has its own tale to tell in this intricate, riveting saga of money.

The Epic Journey of a Coin and a Bill

Ever wondered how money is made and what happens once it's out there in the world? Well, we're about to follow the life of a coin and a bill, from birth to retirement.

First stop on our money journey: the mint. This is where coins are born. Massive machines stamp out coin shapes from sheets of metal. The coins are then inspected, counted, and bagged.

Bills, on the other hand, are born in a printing press. Huge sheets of special paper are printed with the designs we're familiar with. These sheets are then cut into individual bills. It's like a really high-stakes arts and crafts project!

Once the coins and bills are made, they're sent off to banks. And this is where their real journey begins. People withdraw these coins and bills from the bank, and then they start to move around as people spend them.

Imagine if a coin or bill could talk, the stories they would tell! The hot dog they were used to buy at a baseball game, the birthday card they were slipped into as a surprise gift, the piggy bank they were saved in by a kid hoping to buy a new skateboard. They might travel across the city, the country, or even the world, passing from hand to hand, wallet to wallet, till they are worn and tired.

And what happens when they're too old and worn out? They're taken out of circulation. Coins are often melted down to make new ones, and old bills are shredded and sometimes recycled. And that's the end of their journey.

But remember, even as some coins and bills retire, new ones are always being made. It's a never-ending cycle. And every time you use money - to buy something, to save, or to give someone - you're a part of that journey.

So, next time you hold a coin or bill, give a thought to its story and where it might be headed next.

Why Does My Candy Bar Cost More Every Year? Inflation, Revealed

Ever noticed how your grandparents keep telling you about the "good old days" when candy bars were a nickel? If you're wondering why things seem to get more expensive over time, then say hello to your not-so-welcome friend - inflation.

So, what's inflation? Well, in simple terms, it's the rate at which the price of goods and services increases over time. When inflation goes up, every dollar you have buys a smaller percentage of a good or service. It's kind of like how your favorite bag of chips seems to get smaller while the price stays the same, except it's happening to all the stuff you buy.

Now you might be asking, "But why? Why does inflation happen?" Great question! Inflation can happen for several reasons, but one common reason is when there's too much money floating around. If people have more money to spend, businesses might raise prices because they know people can afford to pay a little more. This is called demand-pull inflation.

But there's another type too, called cost-push inflation. This happens when the costs to make goods (like wages or materials) go up. Companies usually don't want to lose money, so they bump up their prices to cover the extra costs.

You might think, "Hey, but if everyone has more money, isn't that a good thing?" Well, not exactly. While having more money can feel great, if prices rise faster than your money, you won't be able to buy as much. That's why some people get a pay raise every year – to keep up with inflation.

And here's another thing: when inflation gets too high, things can get really out of hand. You might have heard stories about places where people had to carry around wheelbarrows full of money to buy a loaf of bread. That's hyperinflation, and trust me, it's no fun.

But don't worry, most countries have clever people in central banks trying to keep inflation just right. Not too high, but also not too low.

Inflation is like a sneaky ghost slowly eating away at the value of your money. It's one of the reasons why it's important to understand money - to keep your hard-earned cash working for you, and not the other way around! So stick around as we learn more about how to handle money.

Deflation: Flipping Inflation on Its Head

Well, guess what? There's an opposite to inflation called deflation.

Deflation is when the average price of goods and services decreases over time. So, instead of prices going up like with inflation, they actually go down. It's like walking into a store and finding that your favorite bag of chips now costs less than it did last year. Sounds awesome, right? Hold your horses - let's dig into this a bit more.

You see, while lower prices might seem like a dream come true, deflation can actually be a bit of a nightmare for the economy. Here's why: if prices keep going down, people might decide to wait to buy things, thinking they'll be even cheaper in the future. This can cause businesses to sell less and less, leading them to cut wages or even let workers go. If this goes on for too long, it can create a vicious cycle that's tough to break.

You might also think, "But if stuff is cheaper, I can buy more, right?" Well, yes, but remember, if businesses are struggling, they might not be able to pay their employees as much, or at all. So, while stuff is cheaper, you might also have less money to spend.

So, who's managing all this inflation and deflation stuff? That would be our central banks. They're like the Goldilocks of the economy - they don't want prices to rise or fall too much. They want it just right. So they adjust things like interest rates to keep the economy balanced. Deflation can be just as tricky to handle as inflation.

Remember, understanding these terms and concepts doesn't just make you sound smart - it also gives you the power to understand the world around you and make informed decisions about your money. So stick around as we dive deeper into these topics. Up next, we'll talk about how countries try to control inflation and deflation.

How Governments Try to Control Inflation and Deflation

Alright, folks, now that we have a grasp on inflation and deflation, it's time to take a look at what the people in charge do to keep them from wreaking havoc in the economy.

You see, governments and central banks have a massive role in managing an economy, kind of like superheroes protecting a city. Except instead of capes and superpowers, they've got policies and regulations. Their main goal? To keep inflation and deflation at just the right level, where the economy can hum along nicely.

So how do they do this? Let's start with inflation. If prices are rising too quickly and our money's losing value faster than a snowman in the sun, then the central bank might step in to slow things down. One way they do this is by raising interest rates. Think of interest rates like the price of borrowing money. If it's more expensive to borrow, people and businesses will likely borrow less, which means less money floating around and therefore, less inflation.

On the other hand, if deflation's the problem and prices are dropping faster than your jaw at the sight of your favorite dessert, then the central bank might lower interest rates to encourage people to spend more.

Sometimes, though, interest rates alone aren't enough. That's when governments step in with their own tools, like changing how much they spend and how much they tax us. If the government spends more money on things like building highways or improving schools, that can stimulate the economy and potentially combat deflation.

Of course, these strategies don't come without risks. It's like a game of balancing on a tightrope: lean too far one way, and you might cause too much inflation; lean too far the other way, and you could end up with deflation. It's a constant balancing act!

It's worth remembering, though, that while these tools can help manage the economy, they're not magic wands. They can't instantly fix everything and sometimes, they can even lead to unintended consequences.

So there you have it, folks! We've taken a whirlwind tour through the world of inflation, deflation, and how our economy's superheroes - I mean, central banks and governments - work to keep things balanced.

But what happens when the world of finance evolves? What happens when new forms of currency, ones not bound by borders or controlled by central banks, start to change the game? That's right, in our next chapter, we're diving into the cutting-edge world of digital money and cryptocurrency. Get ready to discover how these revolutionary concepts could change everything we know about money. Onward to Chapter 3!

Chapter 3 - Digital Money and Cryptocurrencies

C an you recall the last time you pulled out cash from your pocket to pay for something? If you're scratching your head trying to remember, you're not the only one. We're sailing in the same boat, moving away from fishing out wrinkled bills and loose change to swiping and tapping our way through transactions. Welcome to the rise of digital money!

What's steering us from physical to digital money? The answer is simple - it's all about convenience. We live life in the fast lane, always on the move. And digital money fits the bill perfectly for this non-stop lifestyle. Gone are the days of waiting in snaking queues to draw cash from the ATM or scrambling for coins at the cash register. A simple tap, swipe, or click does the trick. And guess what? Your smartphone, your faithful sidekick, doubles as your wallet.

Now, you might be wondering, "Why should I care about digital money?" That's an excellent question, and here's why: it's not just the future—it's now. Digital money isn't some fleeting trend. It's reshaping our lives, from ordering takeout online to sending cash to buddies on the other side of the globe. It's altering how we perceive money—it's more than just digits on a screen. It's a ticket to security, privacy, and financial freedom.

And there's more to digital money than just online banking and payment apps—let's not overlook the thrilling world of cryptocurrencies. You've probably heard whispers about Bitcoin or maybe Ethereum, right? These are digital currencies, that exist entirely online, independent of any government or bank. However, they do have their unique challenges and intricacies. Comprehending them can help you stride confidently into this new territory.

By the time you're done with this chapter, you won't just know what digital money is. You'll know how to use it, how to safeguard it, and even how to invest in it if that's up your alley.

In this tech-saturated world, grasping the concept of digital money is more than a 'nice-to-have' – it's downright essential. So, strap in because we're about to plunge headfirst into the exciting world of digital money.

What is Digital Money?

Alright, we've thrown around the term 'digital money' quite a bit. But what's the real deal? Is it some elusive treasure our parents claimed was just make-believe? Not quite, but it's still pretty rad.

At its core, digital money is just that—money, but make it digital. No physical coins or notes you can hold, fiddle with, or (not that we endorse it) take a taste of. Digital money is all electronic, kind of like the songs you blast or the e-books you devour on your tablet. You can't physically touch them, but they exist, and they're as real as it gets.

Digital money takes on several forms. For starters, we've got credit and debit cards. Odds are, you're no stranger to these. Instead of lugging around stacks of cash, a swipe or a chip insert of a card does the job. This was the first wave of digital money, and it's still riding high today.

Then, enter online banking. It's your personal money manager minus the hassle of visiting a brick-and-mortar bank. You can keep an eye on your account balance, send money around, and even settle your bills from the coziness of your home (or anywhere you've got Wi-Fi).

Next in line, we have mobile payments. It's like cramming your bank and wallet into your smartphone. Apps like Venmo, Cash App, and PayPal transform your device into a money-transmitting wizard. It's as easy as sending a text, but instead of blasting the latest internet craze, you're beaming money.

And lastly, the newbies on the scene: cryptocurrencies. These digital currencies harness cryptography (the techy term for "mega complicated code") to lock up transactions and govern the birth of new units. Bitcoin, the pioneering and most notorious cryptocurrency, is a textbook case. We'll dive deeper into this world a little later.

Now, you might be wondering, "Digital money sounds cool, but it can't be that old, right?" Well, brace yourself, because digital money has been in the game for quite some time. It kicked off in the 1960s with credit cards, ventured into online banking in the '80s, then sprinted into mobile payments in the 2000s. Cryptocurrencies, the most recent recruits, strutted into the spotlight in 2009 with Bitcoin.

So, that's digital money in a nutshell. It's a dynamic concept, shape-shifting and evolving with technology and the pulse of society. It's redesigning our world and the way we engage with money.

Mobile Payments

Remember when we hinted that digital money is like squeezing your wallet into your smartphone? Well, it's time to unravel that a bit. Let's step into the zone of mobile payments.

The Mechanics of Mobile Payments

There's more than one way, but the most popular routes involve Near Field Communication (NFC) and Quick Response (QR) codes.

First off, let's break down NFC. It's a tech that lets two gadgets, like your phone and a payment terminal, chat when they're up close and personal. You might have come across the term "tap-and-go" payments. That's NFC in action. You tap your phone to the terminal, your payment details are zipped over, and bam, you've sorted your bill.

Next up, QR codes. You must have spotted these square designs with all the random lines that you scan with your phone's camera. Certain mobile payment apps harness QR codes to nail transactions. You scan the code, approve the payment on your device, and boom, you're all set!

Top-Notch Mobile Payment Apps

So, what apps can you rely on for mobile payments? There's a smorgasbord, but some of the crowd favorites are Apple Pay, Google Wallet, and Venmo.

Apple Pay and Google Wallet are pretty much twins. They both let you stash your credit or debit card info on your phone and process payments using NFC. They're super convenient for store purchases, and you can even use them for some retail purchases online.

Venmo, on the flip side, is more about money transfers between folks. Need to square up with your buddy for last night's pizza party? Just Venmo them the cash. It's as straightforward as firing off a text message.

Safekeeping with Mobile Payments

Now, I can hear your brain buzzing. "Isn't it a tad risky to have all my payment info on my phone?" And that's a valid concern. But here's the twist: mobile payments are actually pretty secure.

For one, when you execute a mobile payment, your credit or debit card number isn't passed to the seller. Instead, a unique, encrypted number steps in. This means your actual card specifics are kept under wraps.

Additionally, most mobile payment apps come with extra safety nets. For instance, you might need to use a fingerprint, face ID, or PIN to give a transaction the green light. So, even if someone nabbed your phone, they'd hit a brick wall trying to make purchases without your go-ahead.

So there's the lowdown on mobile payments. It's like carrying your wallet, but on steroids. Quicker, safer, and way more convenient.

A Brief Introduction to Cryptocurrencies

So, what on earth are cryptocurrencies? They're digital or virtual currencies that wield cryptography, the craft of scrambling and unscrambling data, for security. Yup, these currencies are super secure, all thanks to the wizardry of math and tech.

Unlike dollars or euros that have governments backing them (we dub these 'fiat currencies'), cryptocurrencies rock and roll on decentralized networks based on blockchain technology. But we'll dive into that later.

Cryptocurrency Origin Story and the Birth of Bitcoin

But where did these cryptocurrencies spring from? To tackle that, we gotta take a leap back to 2009. An incognito person or group, going by the handle Satoshi Nakamoto, hit the scene with Bitcoin, the very first cryptocurrency.

You heard it right, Bitcoin was the trailblazer.

Bitcoin was born out of the 2008 financial meltdown, aiming to deliver a kind of money that doesn't depend on any central bank and can spark instant, cost-friendly payments between folks globally. Since Bitcoin blazed the trail, thousands of spin-off cryptocurrencies, often tagged as 'altcoins', have sprung up, each boasting its own cool features and uses.

The Blockchain Technology Behind Cryptocurrencies

Time to dig a little deeper into what fuels cryptocurrencies - enter Blockchain. Imagine a chain where each link is like a storage box brimming with info. Each box, or 'block', is chock-full of deets about transactions, like who shipped how much cryptocurrency to who. Here's the kicker, once a block is stuffed with info, it's locked down for good - no edits allowed.

This information expressway made up of blocks, hence dubbed 'blockchain', is supervised by a bunch of computers, called 'nodes'. When a shiny new block joins the chain, every node on the network freshens up its blockchain to show off the new addition.

Because this blockchain isn't stashed in a single location but is instead scattered across thousands of nodes, it's super tough to mess with. If someone wanted to twist a transaction, they'd need to outsmart not just one, but thousands of computers all at once!

So, to sum up, cryptocurrencies are a safe, decentralized brand of digital money. It's a wild new world that's miles away from the cash and coins, plastic cards, and even mobile payments we've been chatting about. Mind-blowing, right? Let's dive deeper.

Understanding Bitcoin and Other Cryptocurrencies

Ever felt that tingle of anticipation mixed with a pinch of confusion when you've just unboxed a shiny new gadget? That's pretty much the vibe when Bitcoin and other cryptocurrencies step into the scene. So let's unveil the magic behind these cyber coins, shall we?

Bitcoin Mechanics: The What's What of Wallets, Addresses, Private and Public Keys

Here's the lowdown on Bitcoin. You know how you have a wallet for your cash? Same drill with Bitcoin - you need a 'digital wallet'. But rather than physical coinage or bills, what you're tucking away are two special cryptographic keys: one public and one private.

Think of the public key as your email address. It's what you share so folks can send you Bitcoin. Just like an email, it's up for everyone to see, but only you can sneak a peek at the Bitcoin sent to that address.

The private key, on the other hand, is like your top-secret email password. It's used to access and handle the Bitcoin dropped into your public key. If someone else snags your private key, they can splurge your Bitcoin. So treat that key like a secret diary, alright?

Other Cryptocurrencies: Ethereum, Litecoin, Ripple, and More

Bitcoin might be the big cheese and the most recognized cryptocurrency, but it's got a lot of digital siblings - Ethereum, Litecoin, Ripple, and many more.

Take Ethereum, for example, it's not just another cryptocurrency. It's a complete network with its own web browser, coding language, and payment system. But the real gem here? It enables 'smart contracts', which automatically complete transactions when certain conditions are ticked off.

Litecoin, on the flip side, is like Bitcoin's silver sidekick. It runs on similar lines as Bitcoin but is fine-tuned to make mining (the whole shebang of creating new blocks on the blockchain) faster and cheaper.

Ripple, playing a slightly different game, is both a digital payment protocol and a cryptocurrency. Big businesses and banks tap into the Ripple network to move big money around the globe swiftly and without coughing up hefty fees.

Spotting the Differences Between These Cryptocurrencies

Each cryptocurrency is a unique player but they all root for the same basic principles - cryptography, blockchain tech, and decentralization. However, they vary when it comes to their mission, transaction speed, coin count, and underlying tech.

Bitcoin was conceived as a digital money makeover, while Ethereum was crafted to roll out programmable contracts and apps. Litecoin offers quicker block creation times compared to Bitcoin, and Ripple is all about speed and fitting into the existing banking system.

And there you go - a quick tour of Bitcoin and a few of its digital buddies. We're just nicking the surface here, and the crypto-verse is a whole lot bigger and more fascinating. If this has sparked your curiosity, we'd say it's worth going on a full-blown exploration! Stay tuned for the books, courses and videos we've linked in the resources section at the end of the book.

Investing in Cryptocurrencies

You might have heard the lore of folks morphing into overnight millionaires through crypto investments. Quite the fairy tale, eh? But here's the kicker: investing in cryptocurrencies, like any other investment, swings between risks and rewards. So let's dissect this.

Navigating the Risks and Potential Rewards of Crypto Investments

Cryptocurrencies can make a rollercoaster look like a lazy river ride. One tick you're soaring high, and the next, you're nose-diving. This means that the value of your investment can ricochet wildly in the blink of an eye. The adrenaline rush is legit, but so is the potential for a tumble.

On the sunny side, the potential jackpots can be jaw-dropping. The early birds who caught the Bitcoin worm, for instance, have watched their initial stakes multiply astronomically. And as digital currencies earn their place in the mainstream, some optimists are betting on this upward swing to continue. But, always remember, nothing's chiseled in stone.

Demystifying Cryptocurrency Exchanges

So, how do you actually dip your toes into crypto investments? Say hello to cryptocurrency exchanges. These are platforms that let you buy, sell, or swap cryptocurrencies for other digital goodies or old-school money like dollars or euros.

Imagine them as the Wall Street of digital money. You sign up for an account, unload your traditional dollars or other cryptocurrencies, and then you're set to start trading. Some of the big-league exchanges include Coinbase, Binance, and Kraken.

The Crucial Role of Security in the Crypto-Verse

Before you jump onto the crypto investment bandwagon, there's a golden rule you should never forget: security. In the digital arena, danger lurks around every corner, including hackers on the prowl to loot your precious digital coins.

That's why you should always have your coins tucked away securely. Many investors bank on digital wallets, which can be hardware-based or online, to stash their cryptocurrencies. Also, don't skimp on strong passwords, and make sure to switch on any extra security features dished out by the exchange, like two-factor authentication.

Just as you wouldn't leave your purse or wallet for someone to snag, treat your digital wallet with the same vigilance. After all, your painstakingly earned digital coins deserve a safe haven, right?

To wrap it up, the crypto universe is bursting with thrilling prospects, but it's not a risk-free joyride. So, if you're toying with the idea of joining the game, ensure you're armed with ample knowledge and buckle up for a wild ride!

Cryptocurrencies and the Law

The intriguing narrative of cryptocurrencies is incomplete without acknowledging their relationship, often tumultuous, with the law. Let's plunge right in...

The Legal Mosaic of Cryptocurrencies Across the Globe

Firstly, it's essential to recognize that the legal status of cryptocurrencies is as diverse as the world's cultures. In some territories, like Japan and Switzerland, cryptocurrencies are given a warm welcome and treated much like conventional forms of currency. In these nations, everything from a morning espresso to a shiny new car can be purchased with Bitcoin.

Conversely, some nations, including China and India, have rolled out stringent regulations or flat-out bans on cryptocurrencies. They point to concerns about financial stability, the threat of fraud, and the potential undermining of their national currencies.

Then, there are the countries in the middle ground, like the United States and the European Union, where cryptocurrencies are neither outlawed nor entirely mainstream. They're often viewed more as an investment asset rather than bona fide money. Hence, depending on your geographical location, using Bitcoin could be as easy as pie, illegal, or somewhere in between!

Cryptocurrencies and the Underworld

Now, let's delve into the murkier waters. Due to the anonymity that cryptocurrencies offer, they've occasionally been exploited for illicit activities such as money laundering and purchasing illegal commodities online. The anonymity makes these transactions tougher (but not impossible) to trace for authorities.

However, it's important to underline that the vast majority of cryptocurrency users are not engaged in illegal activities. Like any tool, it's not about the tool itself but its application.

Regulation in the Cryptocurrency Sphere

You've probably heard the phrase that cryptocurrencies are 'unregulated.' There's some truth in that. Compared to conventional financial systems, the cryptocurrency world operates with less supervision. But that's not to say it's entirely lawless.

Governments and international entities are gradually crafting regulations to incorporate cryptocurrencies into mainstream financial systems while attempting to control the risks. This includes measures like enforcing identity verification on exchanges to thwart money laundering.

However, it's a fine line. Over-regulation could potentially strangle innovation and the benefits that cryptocurrencies can offer, while under-regulation could leave users defenseless and expose financial risks.

In summary, the crossroads of cryptocurrencies and the law is a complex and rapidly evolving landscape. It adds another layer of complexity when contemplating entering the realm of digital currency. As always, knowledge is your most potent weapon!

Gazing into the Crystal Ball: The Future of Digital Money and Cryptocurrencies

We've dissected what digital money and cryptocurrencies are and their mechanisms, right? Now, let's take a leap into the future. Hold your breath, because the world of digital money is just warming up!

Up-and-Coming Trends in Digital Money

First on the list are Central Bank Digital Currencies (CBDCs). Recollect the conventional money we've used for eons? Central banks globally are now toying with the concept of issuing digital renditions of this money. Picture a digital dollar or a digital euro issued directly by the central bank. It could combine the ease and efficiency of cryptocurrencies while maintaining the reliability and stability of traditional money.

Next, we've got non-fungible tokens (NFTs). These unique digital assets utilize blockchain technology (yep, the same tech backing Bitcoin). However, unlike Bitcoin, each NFT is utterly unique. Consider them akin to digital collectibles or digital artwork. They've caused quite the stir in the realms of art, music, and gaming.

Finally, there's decentralized finance, or DeFi for short. This revolutionary way of conducting finance omits traditional intermediaries like banks and instead relies on smart contracts on a blockchain. It facilitates functions like lending, borrowing, and earning interest in a more transparent and accessible way.

How These Trends Could Reshape Everyday Life

Now, you may be asking, "How does this impact me?" Well, these advancements could revolutionize our daily lives in ways you couldn't possibly imagine.

Imagine a future where you can dispatch digital dollars as effortlessly as a text message, straight from your smartphone, at any hour, to anyone across the globe. Or where you can purchase and sell unique digital collectibles, like a virtual trading card or digital artwork. Or where you can access financial services not from a bank, but from a decentralized network that's accessible to anyone with an internet connection.

Of course, like anything novel, these trends bring their own set of challenges and risks. For instance, CBDCs could raise privacy concerns, NFTs have been criticized for their environmental impact, and DeFi grapples with issues surrounding security and regulation.

But regardless of whether we're ready or not, the world of money is evolving. The more we understand about these changes, the better equipped we'll be to navigate this thrilling, occasionally bewildering, but ultimately empowering digital landscape.

But do keep this in mind: this isn't just about being proficient enough to use Bitcoin for a pizza delivery or reimbursing your pals for a movie night via Venmo. This is about comprehending the monumental shift occurring in our economy and society. Digital currencies and cryptocurrencies are not just trending tech; they're altering how we conceptualize and interact with money.

The kicker is, it's all still developing. The domain of digital money is akin to an ever-evolving video game, continuously updated with new features, challenges, and opportunities. So keep enriching your knowledge and stay open to continuous learning.

So, what's the next step? Perhaps channel your newfound understanding into action? You might want to venture into setting up a mobile payment app to share expenses with friends or family. Or, if you're feeling bold, you might even consider venturing into the realm of cryptocurrencies by setting up a crypto wallet. Remember to tread carefully and responsibly - this world is as fraught with risks as it is with excitement.

Well, that brings us to the end of our deep dive into the world of digital money and cryptocurrencies. But don't put your thinking caps away just yet! As we turn the page, you'll find an exciting quiz waiting to test your newfound financial wisdom. 'Read, Set, Recall' isn't just about checking your retention; it's also a fantastic tool to help solidify these key concepts in your mind. So, are you ready to recap, revise, and refresh your knowledge? Let's leap into the final chapter of Part 1!

Ready, Set, Recall

Time to hit pause and do a quick check-in on all the awesome stuff you've soaked up in this part. No stress if you don't nail every question right away. This is your chance to recap and reinforce what you've learned.

You'll find the answer key at the end of the resources chapter of the book (no peeking!). Ready?

1. What's the key reason we can't live without money?
    A. Money is shiny.
    B. Money is a universal medium of exchange.
    C. Money makes us happy.
    D. Money grows on trees.

2. Which of the following plays a crucial role in determining the value of money?
    A. The type of paper used in printing
    B. The trust that people place in it
    C. The size of the coins
    D. The number of zeros on a bill

3. Why does your candy bar cost more every year?
    A. Because candy is becoming rare

B. Because of inflation

C. Because the candy company is greedy

D. Because your allowance increased

4. What happens during deflation?

    A. The cost of goods and services increases.

    B. The cost of goods and services decreases.

    C. The government prints more money.

    D. Cryptocurrencies become more popular.

5. How do governments typically try to control inflation?

    A. By changing interest rates

    B. By printing more money

    C. By adjusting the price of candy bars

    D. By banning the use of cryptocurrencies

6. What is digital money?

    A. Money with digital images on it

    B. Virtual currency that exists only in the digital world

    C. A type of rare coin

    D. Paper money that has been scanned and stored on a computer

7. What technology underlies most cryptocurrencies?

    A. The Internet

    B. Digital scanners

    C. Blockchain technology

    D. Quantum computing

8. What was the first and the most well-known cryptocurrency?

    A. Dogecoin

    B. Ether

    C. Bitcoin

    D. Dollarcoin

9. Is it legal to invest in cryptocurrencies?

    A. Yes, in all circumstances

    B. No, it's illegal everywhere

    C. It depends on the laws of the country you are in

    D. Only if you are over 21

10. What is one way you can use digital money?

    A. By throwing it into a wishing well

    B. For mobile payments

    C. As a bookmark

    D. To play Monopoly

II

Part 2 - Banknotes to Paychecks: A Journey Through Finance and Careers

Chapter 4 - Banks Unzipped: The Inside Scoop

Banking Basics: Getting Down to Brass Tacks

Okay, let's break this down. A bank - what is it, really? Well, it's not just a stuffy place where grown-ups go and stand in line. Think of it as a giant, secure vault where people keep their money. But it's not only about safeguarding our precious coins and notes. Banks have a pretty key role in our daily lives and how our society ticks along, and that's why they're around.

Now, how about a quick time travel to understand where banks came from? You might be surprised to learn that the earliest banks weren't banks at all—they were temples! Yep, back in ancient times, folks would leave their valuables in temples, trusting the priests to keep them safe. Move the timeline to the Middle Ages, and goldsmiths stepped in. They worked with valuable metals, so people figured they'd be trustworthy with their money too.

Over centuries, banking has transformed, growing way more complex. Nowadays, banks do so much more than just store money. They lend it out to people, too—for all sorts of reasons like buying a home, setting up a business, or funding education. And they also make it easier for us to buy and sell things.

Fancy a new video game from an online store? Thanks to banks, you can get it without physically handing over stacks of bills or bags of coins.

In short, banks wear quite a few hats. They keep our money safe, they help us fund our dreams, and they make buying and selling stuff a whole lot smoother.

Whether it's a mega bank with offices around the globe or a tiny local bank that serves a small town, each one plays a crucial part in keeping our economy rolling. And just like understanding money itself, getting to grips with how banks work can give you a major head start in mastering your finances.

So, get ready as we're about to delve deeper into the world of banking.

Interest Rates: The Key to Money Multiplication

Picture this – you've got a $100 and you want it to grow, but you're not keen on doing any heavy lifting. What's the game plan? Well, you could hide it under your mattress, but spoiler alert: it's not gonna sprout extra dollars. Or, you could pop it into a bank that gives you interest. Now, that's where the fun begins.

Interest is like the thank you gift that banks give you for trusting them with your wealth. This thank you is a little extra money – a percentage of the cash you've stored with them – and it's added back into your account, making your total stash grow. It's like you've planted a money tree – your tree (your money) sprouts a bit each year (interest), boosting what you initially planted.

But here's the kicker – not all banks or bank accounts offer the same interest rates. It's like hunting for the best bargain. So, always remember to compare interest rates before you choose where to park your dough.

Now, here's the twist – interest rates can flip. They're kinda like a roller-coaster, climbing and dipping based on a bunch of factors. These factors include how the economy's doing its dance and decisions spun by the central bank.

When the economy's strutting its stuff, interest rates usually shimmy up. But when the economy's feeling a bit low, rates usually slide down. It's a bit of a tightrope walk to keep the economy steady.

Oh, and here's another nugget – different types of bank accounts can have different interest rates too. Savings accounts usually offer higher interest rates than checking accounts. That's why they're the go-to for money you're aiming to grow over time.

Interest rates might seem like a brain-teaser at first, but once you get the hang of it, you'll see how they can work some serious magic on your money. Now, isn't that a bit spellbinding?

Alright, let's flip this money chat and check out the other side. We've been talking about how banks can help you grow your money, but how do banks actually rake in the cash?

How do Banks Make Their Money?

Interest from Lending Out Money

You've probably pieced this together by now – banks rake in a hefty slice of their money through something called interest. But wait, didn't we say you earn interest on your deposits? Yup, we did. But here's the kicker – banks also slap on interest, but they do it in a whole different way – they charge interest on the cash they give out as loans.

Imagine for a second that you're running a bank. You're sitting on a stash of deposits from folks who believe in you to keep their hard-earned money safe. It's like your piggy bank of available funds. Suddenly, someone strides in needing a loan, maybe to buy their dream house or kick off a start-up. They dip into your piggy bank of funds, promising to pay you back, with a cherry on top. That cherry is the interest, and it's one of the main ways banks keep the cash flowing in.

Avalanche of Fees

Next on the list, banks also fill their coffers through a bunch of fees. You know, those annoying little charges that sneak up for certain services, like keeping an account, using an ATM, or sending cash overseas. These fees are another juicy stream of income for banks. Kinda like a movie theater charging you an arm and a leg for popcorn and soda – it's an extra way for them to earn a buck besides the main event (or, in this case, dishing out loans).

Loans, Credit, and the Cash Carousel

Loans and credit form another big piece of the banking puzzle. You've probably heard the term "credit" tossed around. In the world of banking, credit is essentially a loan – it's cash given out on a pinky-promise that it'll be paid back, usually with a side of interest.

Banks are like a spinning cash carousel. They scoop up deposits, hand out that money as loans and credit, earn interest on those loans, and then sprinkle a part of that interest back to the depositors. It's a cycle that keeps the bank's wheels turning and allows it to keep serving up its services.

And there you go! Banks might seem like wizards pulling money out of a hat, but the magic is actually a system of lending, interest, and fees that keeps their engine humming. As you blaze your financial trail, it's always a smart move to remember how this system spins!

Exploring Different Bank Account Types: Checking, Savings, Money Market Accounts, and Certificates of Deposit (CDs)

Checking Accounts

Alright, picture this: you need to stash your money somewhere safe, and preferably somewhere it's always at hand whenever you need it. Enter the checking account. It's like your money's favorite lounge spot, providing a secure place to chill while also being super reachable.

What's So Great About Checking Accounts?

1. Accessibility: One of the best things about checking accounts is their user-friendliness. You can grab your cash pretty much anytime you want, as often as you want. Whether you're snagging the latest issue of your top comic online or calling up a double pepperoni pizza for gaming night, your debit card or checkbook has your back.

2. Online Banking and Apps: Most banks these days have apps where you can check your balance, shuffle money around, or pay bills. It's like carrying a mini bank in your pocket, which is pretty darn cool if you ask me.

3. Safety: Stashing your cash in a checking account is way safer than hiding it under your mattress or in a random shoebox. Banks are like high-security vaults, and they're also insured, so even if something truly bananas happened (think zombie apocalypse), your money would be safe.

But what's the catch?

1. Fees: Some checking accounts come with pesky fees. These might be monthly fees, or charges for things like using an ATM from a different bank.

So, always remember to read the fine print and understand any fees you might have to cough up.

2. Low or No Interest: While some checking accounts do earn a smidge of interest, most don't. This means your money isn't sprouting extra greenbacks over time like it would in a savings account or a CD (certificates of deposit).

3. Overdrafts: If you splurge more cash than you have in your account, you'll hit an overdraft. That means you're in debt to the bank, and they'll usually slap you with an extra fee for that. It's like a penalty for spending cash you didn't have.

In the end, a checking account is all about convenience. It's like your money's personal superhero, ready to swoop in for everyday expenses. But remember, it's not a magic wand, and the golden rules of wise spending still apply.

Savings Accounts

Picture yourself as a squirrel, stockpiling acorns for winter. You wouldn't munch on them immediately, right? Instead, you'd squirrel them away in a hole, ready for when the snow starts falling. That's basically the concept of a savings account.

So, what's so awesome about Savings Accounts?

1. Growing Your Cash: When you deposit your money into a savings account, it doesn't just lounge around. It actually blossoms over time thanks to interest. Think of it as a mini high-five from the bank for trusting them with your money.

2. Safety: Just as with checking accounts, your cash is super secure in a savings account. The bank's got the security angle covered, and the government insures your money.

3. Saving for Goals: Dreaming of saving up for something amazing, like a shiny new skateboard, a state-of-the-art gadget, or perhaps a dream trip? A savings account is a fab place to keep that money snug and let it fatten up while you're hustling towards your goal.

And the downsides?

1. Limited Withdrawals: Savings accounts are designed for stashing, not splurging. That's why banks put a cap on how many times you can dip into your savings each month. If you reach in too often, you could face a fee.

2. Minimum Balance Requirements: Some savings accounts ask you to maintain a certain amount of money in them. If your balance drops below that minimum, you could end up paying a fee.

3. Lower Interest Rates: While savings accounts do earn interest, the rates are often on the low side compared to other investments. It's like a trade-off for the safety and easy access they offer.

Think of a savings account as a snug burrow for your future dreams. It's a place where your money can chill, safe and sound, while slowly bulking up.

Money Market Accounts

Picture a Money Market Account (MMA for short), as a dynamic duo superhero - it possesses the sweet traits of a checking account, alongside the solid virtues of a savings account. It's basically the ultimate two-in-one package.

So what are the advantages of Money Market Accounts?

1. Interest Rates: MMAs generally offer interest rates that outrank regular savings accounts. That equates to your money beefing up at a quicker pace. Think of it as your cash having VIP access to the express lane.

2. Access to Your Money: MMAs often come with the bonus of check-writing and debit card usage. Need to shell out some dough for something? No sweat, your MMA has got your back.

3. Safety: Aligning with the norms of checking and savings accounts, MMAs are covered by government insurance. Your money is as guarded as if it were stashed away in a top-tier secure vault.

Okay, what's the downside?

1. Minimum Balance Requirement: MMAs often demand a steeper minimum balance compared to regular savings accounts. If you don't uphold that minimum, you might be slapped with fees, or your interest rate might experience a slump.

2. Limited Transactions: Even though you get the perks of checks and a debit card with MMAs, there's a cap on how many transactions you can make each month. If you cross that limit, you might be hit with a fee.

3. Not Always the Highest Returns: While MMAs often flaunt higher rates than savings accounts, there are other investment avenues that can yield higher returns. So it's all about weighing your options and choosing what's best for you and your financial game plan.

Money Market Accounts are like an extraordinary hybrid, fusing some stellar features of both checking and savings accounts. They could be the perfect match for you, or perhaps not. It all hinges on your unique needs and aspirations.

Certificates of Deposit (CDs)

Think of CDs as the enduring marathon runners in the banking world. Unlike checking accounts, savings accounts, and money market accounts, which let you access your money relatively easily, CDs ask you to promise not to touch your money for a while. In return, they typically offer higher interest rates, helping your savings grow even more over time. It's a different approach, but it can be a real winner.

Here's the cool stuff about CDs:

1. Interest Rates: CDs generally offer higher interest rates compared to your regular savings or money market accounts. That means the cash you tuck away in a CD will bulk up at a speedier pace. Picture it like sowing a seed and observing it bloom into a robust tree over time.

2. Safety: CDs have the security stamp of government insurance, which translates to your money being in a super safe zone. It's akin to locking your cash in a safety deposit box that also nurtures its growth.

Alright, what's the twist with CDs?:

1. Time Commitment: When you commit your money to a CD, you're giving a word to the bank to let it stay put for a certain fixed duration. This can range anywhere from a couple of months to several years. Consider it a pact with your bank: "I'll lend you my money for a stipulated period, and in return, you'll foster its growth."

2. Early Withdrawal Penalties: If you have to withdraw your money from the CD before its maturity date (that's the end of your agreed time period), you'll generally be slapped with a penalty. So, CDs are an ideal pick if you're confident that you won't require the money in the near future.

3. Inflation Risk: Although CDs can nurture your money's growth, if the interest rate of your CD lags behind the inflation rate, you might end up losing purchasing power over time. In layman's terms, your money might not go as far when it comes to shopping.

So, that's the rundown! CDs are a fantastic choice for those who are certain they can leave their money untouched for a while, and would like to witness consistent growth. They're like marathon runners, unhurried yet persistent, and hey, they often bag the prize in the long run.

Alright, my money-savvy friends, that's the rundown on banks - your one-stop shops for money storage, borrowing, and a whole lot more. We've toured their inner workings, explored the variety of services they provide, and shed light on their crucial role in our economy. Banks aren't just vaults filled with cash; they're key players in our financial world, and knowing how they operate gives us the power to navigate that world confidently.

But let's not rest on our laurels just yet. With this newfound knowledge, we're equipped to dive into the exciting realm of income generation - the art and science of money-making. Whether it's through a part-time gig, a full-blown career, or creative passive income avenues, there's a multitude of ways to earn, save, and grow your cash.

So, buckle up, because we're about to shift gears from understanding how money is kept to discovering how it's made. See you in the next chapter!

Chapter 5 - Income Generation: How To Make Money!

Unpacking the Concepts of Income: Active versus Passive

Here's the kicker - income doesn't follow a 'one size fits all' approach. We're primarily dealing with two kinds - active and passive income. Let's untangle this.

Active income - this represents the funds you accumulate when you're squarely in the fray, laboring diligently. Essentially, it's like your conventional job. You're present, navigating the daily grind, and lo and behold, your paycheck arrives. You're actively exchanging hours for money, thus the term 'active' income.

Then, there's this intriguing phenomenon called passive income. This is akin to generating money while in leisure mode. You're not actively toiling for it, but the dollars continue to stream in. For instance, consider you're a songwriter. You compose an appealing melody once, and then every instance it's broadcasted on the radio, you get paid. Sounds delightful, doesn't it? But hold your horses, it's not always smooth sailing, but we'll touch on that later.

Elements Influencing Income Generation: Education, Skills, Experience,

and Location

Now, the quantum of money you garner isn't arbitrary. There's a certain logic to it, and a multitude of factors can sway it.

First in line, is education. In our society, knowledge wields influence - and frequently, influence equates to financial gain. The higher your educational attainments, such as degrees or diplomas, the larger your potential income (in many cases, but not always!). Consider professions like doctors or lawyers - their educational journey is prolonged, but upon completion, their paychecks mirror that.

Following this, we have skills and experience. The more adept and seasoned you are at a task, the higher your likely remuneration. Draw a comparison between a master chef and a novice - who do you suppose earns more?

Finally, there's the geographical aspect. Analogous to how a house's cost might fluctuate from one locale to another, your income can alter based on your living conditions. A technology professional in a technologically advanced city might outearn someone in the same role in a smaller town.

Keep in mind, income isn't solely about the quantum you generate. It's about grasping how you accrue it, and what influences that. Consider it a blueprint to your financial future - once you comprehend it, you're holding the reins!

Active Income: Earnings from Work

The Concept of Trading Time and Skills for Money

What's up, future money-makers? Let's get into the nitty-gritty of the most common way folks make money: active income. This is about being in the game, front and center. Trading your time and skills for money. Imagine it like a time shop. You clock in, spend some time serving up your brainpower, your talent, or your muscles, and in return, you get cold, hard cash.

You might be asking, "What if I'm flipping burgers, coding software, or saving lives as a paramedic?" Yep, you got it! All those gigs fall under active income. If you're trading hours from your day to get paid, then it's active income, no matter what you're doing.

Common Forms of Active Income: Salaries, Wages, Tips, and Commissions

Now, active income has a few different faces. The most common ones are salaries, wages, tips, and commissions.

A salary is when you get a set amount of money every year, no matter how much or how little you work. It's like the deluxe box set of income - everything's included.

On the other hand, wages are like the "pay-as-you-go" option. You're getting paid for each hour you work. You clock in more hours, you get more bucks.

Tips and commissions, they're the cherries on top. Tips are those extra dollars customers give for good service, while commissions are a slice of the pie from every sale you make. These can make a nice bonus to your regular income.

Potential for income growth and career progression

Now, active income isn't just about making money today. It's also about looking ahead to future paydays. As you gain more skills and experience, your income can grow. That's what we call a raise. And as you climb the ladder at work (hello, promotions!), your income can go from "Alright" to "Awesome!"

Remember, making money isn't just about the here and now. It's also about investing time and effort into your future self. The time and skills you're trading today can turn into bigger and better opportunities tomorrow. So, keep leveling up, and watch your active income grow along with you!

Career Choices and Income Potential

The Relationship Between Career Choice and Potential Income

Let's dive into something pretty important: how the career you choose can impact your potential income. It's kinda like picking a player in a video game, each with its own set of superpowers and challenges.

Some careers are like high-speed trains—full throttle, straight into a hefty paycheck. Think tech geniuses in Silicon Valley or top-tier lawyers in the big city. But others? They're more like those chugging little steam trains. They might not pay a million bucks, but they're packed with passion and personal reward. Like artists, teachers, or nonprofit workers.

Here's the key: every career has its unique value. You've gotta weigh up what's important to you—passion, purpose, lifestyle, or high income—and make your choices accordingly.

Impact of Industry Trends and Economic Factors on Income Potential

Just like weather forecasts and fashion trends, industries change too. So, it's smart to keep an eye on what's going on in the big, wide world of work.

Some industries are booming with high-income jobs right now. Think cybersecurity, AI, and renewable energy. Others might be taking a hit from stuff like automation or economic downturns.

The secret sauce is being adaptable, right? As the world changes, so do job opportunities and income potential. So, always be ready to learn new skills or even switch lanes if you have to.

Discussion on Income Disparities Across Different Careers and Sectors

Now, let's get real. Not all careers are created equal when it comes to income. And it's not just about different jobs. It's also about the sectors and industries they're in.

For instance, a software engineer at a major tech company might earn a lot more than an engineer designing equipment for a small manufacturing company. Or a nurse working in a specialist hospital unit might bring in more than one in a community health center.

Even within the same job, there might be disparities. Think about the gender pay gap and other types of wage discrimination that, unfortunately, still exist.

Remember, knowledge is power. Being aware of these disparities can help you make informed decisions about your career path and stand up for fair pay when it's your turn to negotiate that paycheck.

Keep these things in mind, as they can make a big difference in your financial journey. Remember, while income is important, it's not the only thing that matters. Do what you love, value your work, and the money will follow.

Passive Income: Money While You Sleep

Understanding the Concept of Passive Income

So, you're familiar with the idea of working for your money. But what about your money working for you? Pretty cool thought, right? That's the magic of passive income - it's like having little dollar minions out there hustling for you while you chill or even sleep.

In simple terms, passive income is money you earn with little to no daily effort. It doesn't mean there's no work involved at all, but the idea is you do the hard yards upfront, and then the cash keeps rolling in with minimal upkeep.

Examples of Passive Income: Investments, Rental Income, Royalties, Online Businesses, Etc.

Want to know how to set up your own team of dollar minions? Let's go through some popular forms of passive income.

First up, investments. You might've heard of stocks, bonds, or even real estate investment. Basically, you're putting your money into something that you expect will grow or give you returns over time.

Next, rental income. Got an extra room, a granny flat, or a whole house you're not using? Rent it out, and you're sitting on a potential goldmine.

Royalties are another cool way to earn passive income. Are you a songwriter, author, or inventor? Every time someone buys your song, book, or patented product, you get a cut.

And don't forget online businesses. You can start a blog, create an online course, or set up an e-commerce store. Once they're up and running, they could keep making money even while you're in dreamland.

Pros and Cons of Pursuing Passive Income Streams

Before you rush off to start your blog or buy your first stocks, it's worth noting that passive income streams have their pros and cons.

On the bright side, passive income can give you more financial freedom and flexibility. It can make your wallet heavier without requiring a 9-5 commitment. Plus, it's exciting! Who doesn't want to see their bank account grow while binging their favorite series?

But hold up, it's not all sunshine and rainbows. Setting up a passive income stream usually needs some upfront investment, either of time, money, or often both. And it might take a while before you see any returns. Plus, there's always some risk involved. Investments can go down as well as up, and online businesses can flop.

But hey, don't let the potential pitfalls scare you. Instead, see them as challenges to navigate. Just remember to do your research, make smart decisions, and have a plan in place. And then? Who knows, you might just wake up one day to find your dollar minions have been hard at work!

Weighing Active and Passive Income

The Role of Active and Passive Income in Wealth Generation

Alright, so we've chatted about active income (the 'show up and get paid' kind), and passive income (the 'money minions at work' kind). Both have a place in the grand game of wealth generation, but they play different roles.

Think of active income as your sturdy base camp. It's reliable, it's steady, and it pays the bills. This is the money you're earning from your job, where you trade your time and skills for cash. It's super important because it keeps you afloat and allows you to take care of your basic needs and responsibilities.

Now, passive income, that's like the rocket fuel for your financial journey. While active income is limited by the number of hours you can work in a day, passive income has no such boundaries. It's scalable, meaning there's no limit to how much you can earn. The more successful your passive income ventures are, the faster you can build wealth.

Balancing Active Work and Passive Income Strategies

But how do you strike a balance between active work and passive income strategies? Think of it as a seesaw. When you're starting out, the active income side will be heavier. But as you begin to explore passive income opportunities, invest your money wisely, and see returns, the seesaw gradually levels out.

It's important to remember that generating passive income isn't an overnight thing. It requires time, effort, and sometimes upfront capital. While you're building these income streams, your active income is what keeps you going.

How Diversifying Income Streams Can Enhance Financial Stability

You've probably heard the saying, "Don't put all your eggs in one basket." This sage advice definitely applies to income generation too. Having different income streams - some active, some passive - can give you financial stability.

Why? Because let's face it, life is unpredictable. You might lose your job, your rental property might stay vacant for a couple of months, or your investments might take a hit. If you're relying on just one source of income, any disruption can cause financial stress. But if you have multiple streams, you're better insulated against these financial shocks.

Diversifying your income streams is a bit like having a financial safety net. It doesn't just protect you if things go south, it also opens up opportunities for financial growth. More income streams mean more ways for your money to work for you, giving you the freedom to build your wealth, follow your passions, and navigate your financial journey with confidence.

Income Generation in the Digital Age

The Impact of Technology on Income Opportunities

Okay, time to chat about something super cool - the Digital Age. We're living in a time where we can carry a mini-computer (yeah, your smartphone) in our pocket. It's a magical time when earning opportunities are no longer bound by geographical location or traditional work hours. Exciting, right?

Thanks to technology, there's an incredible array of new income opportunities just a click or tap away. From online jobs to digital entrepreneurship, the digital realm is a treasure trove of earning potential. These are jobs and businesses you can run from your laptop or even your phone, whether you're in your bedroom or chilling at a beach halfway across the world (given you've got a decent internet connection).

And it's not just about convenience. Online jobs can open doors to industries or roles that might be scarce in your local area. And digital entrepreneurship? That's a whole new frontier for innovation and business creation. This digital revolution is transforming the way we think about work and income.

Potential Income Sources Unique to the Digital Age

Alright, let's zoom in on some of the specific income sources that are unique to the Digital Age. Ever heard of content creation? If you're an expert or passionate about a topic (yes, even if that topic is just your own life), you can earn money by creating and sharing content online.

Whether it's YouTube videos, blog posts, podcasts, or Instagram photos, there's a global audience out there ready to consume your content. And where there's an audience, there's a potential for income. This could come in the form of ad revenue, brand partnerships, or even fan donations on platforms like Patreon.

Then there's affiliate marketing, where you promote other people's products and earn a commission on any sales made through your referral links. It's like being a digital salesperson. You can start by recommending products you genuinely love and use to your online following. And guess what? Each sale that comes through your link is money in your pocket.

These are just a couple of examples of digital income sources. The online world is bustling with opportunities, from selling products on an online store to offering freelance services. The Digital Age has truly revolutionized income generation, offering exciting new ways to earn money beyond traditional employment. The world is your digital oyster!

Now, I want you to keep in mind that there's no one-size-fits-all path to financial wellness. Your journey will be as unique as you are, so it's essential to stay open-minded. Explore, experiment, and be creative with your income generation strategies. It's okay to try different things until you find what works best for you.

Remember, financial wellness isn't about how much money you make. It's about how you manage what you have, and how you plan for the future. As long as you're actively working towards a better financial future, you're on the right track.

So, what's next? It's time to take action! Start exploring different income streams. Look at your skills, passions, and interests. How can they translate into earning opportunities?

Consider different career paths. Maybe there's a high-demand industry that aligns with your interests. Or perhaps you're intrigued by the idea of earning passive income through investments or online businesses.

If you're curious about finding the right career path for you, be sure to read our book The Essential Career Planning Handbook for Teens to get you started on the right track.

And most importantly, never stop learning. The world of income generation is vast and ever-changing.

Chapter 6 - Basics of Taxes and Understanding Your Paycheck

Taxes. You've probably heard adults groaning about them, seen lines on your receipt labeled 'tax,' or maybe even had a chunk of your first paycheck seem to mysteriously disappear. Taxes are pretty much like homework, not always fun but necessary. It's how governments raise money to fund public services, like roads, schools, and healthcare. It's like a communal piggy bank where everyone chips in for the greater good.

Understanding taxes isn't just about being a responsible adult. It's about grasping how the world works and how you contribute to it. The truth is, even if taxes seem daunting, they're not some indecipherable mystery; they're just a part of our everyday lives. So, gear up, because we're going on a journey to demystify the world of taxes.

A Quick Travel Through Time: History of Taxation

Let's take a trip in our time machine. Did you know taxes have been around for thousands of years? It's true! They were even a part of ancient civilizations. The Egyptians paid taxes in the form of grain, the Romans paid a wealth tax to fund their armies, and in Medieval Europe, people had to give a tenth of their earnings to the church, known as a tithe.

As societies grew more complex, so did the tax systems. Over time, governments started collecting taxes in the form of money. These funds were used for public works, security, and sometimes, for the rulers' lavish lifestyles. The tax system we have today, albeit not perfect, has been refined over centuries and is continually evolving to fit our changing society.

The Many Faces of Taxes: Income, Sales, Property, and More

Today, there are several types of taxes, each with its own rules. Here's a quick run-down:

Income tax: This is probably the one you're most familiar with. It's the tax levied on your earnings, whether from a job, a business, or investments.

Sales tax: Ever wonder why the price at the checkout counter is more than the tag on the item? That's sales tax. It's added to the cost of goods and services and varies from state to state.

Property tax: If you own property, like a house, you'll have to pay property taxes. These funds usually go to local governments to pay for things like public schools and law enforcement.

Of course, there are many other types of taxes, but these are the big ones you'll likely encounter in your day-to-day life.

By the end of this chapter, you'll be much more tax savvy. So, let's keep the momentum going!

The Paycheck Breakdown

Gross Pay vs Net Pay: Unmasking the Mystery

So you've snagged your first job and can't wait to get your hands on that paycheck. You've done the math and have already dreamt up ways to spend your hard-earned money. But then, boom! The paycheck arrives, and it's not the number you were waiting for. Welcome to the world of gross pay vs net pay.

Here's the scoop: gross pay is the big number you first heard when you got the job offer. It's your full, untouched earnings. Net pay, on the other hand, is the money that finally makes its way to your bank account. What happens in between? The answer, my friend, is deductions.

Common Deductions: The Culprits Behind Your Shrinking Paycheck

Okay, so now you know why your net pay is less than your gross pay. But what exactly are these deductions that make such a big difference? Let's get to know them better:

Federal and state income tax: No matter where you're earning, some of your money goes towards income tax. The exact amount depends on your income and the state you live in.

Social Security tax: This is your contribution to a pool of funds that supports older adults, people with disabilities, and families with retired, disabled, or deceased workers.

Medicare tax: This small slice of your paycheck goes towards providing healthcare for people who are 65 or older or who have certain disabilities.

Remember, while these deductions may reduce your take-home pay, they're doing important work for you and others.

Voluntary Deductions: It's Your Call!

There's another type of deduction that might pop up on your paycheck: voluntary deductions. As the name suggests, these are the ones you opt into. They could include:

Retirement contributions: If your workplace has a retirement plan, you can choose to pay into it straight from your paycheck.

Health insurance: If your job offers health insurance, your share of the premium may be deducted from your pay.

Even though these deductions may initially sting a little, remember they're for your benefit in the long run.

W-2 Form: Your Yearly Payroll Recap

Once a year, your employer sends you a "W-2 form". It's like a yearbook for your job – a summary of all your earnings and deductions over the past year.

The W-2 might look like a puzzle at first, with all its boxes and numbers. But it's actually breaking down your income, taxes withheld, and contributions to Social Security and Medicare. It's key to filing your taxes, so keep it safe!

By the end of this chapter, you'll be a paycheck decoding master. It's a real-world skill that'll set you up for success. So, stay tuned and enjoy this learning journey!

Income Tax Basics

What Counts as Income? Your Taxable Income Explained

Now, here's the kicker: not every dollar you earn counts as income for tax purposes. The government only taxes what they call your "taxable income." Sounds mysterious? It's actually pretty straightforward. Your taxable income includes money you earn from working, certain types of interest and dividends from investments, and a few other sources. But it's not just money – certain non-cash benefits (think company car or a sweet apartment your job provides) can count as income too!

Figuring out your taxable income involves subtracting certain amounts, like specific deductions, from your total income. This gives you the amount you'll actually be taxed on. Don't worry, we'll dive into that a bit later!

The Progressive Nature of Income Tax: Climbing the Tax Bracket Ladder

Now, let's talk about how your taxable income translates into the actual tax you owe. In the U.S, we have a "progressive" tax system. No, it's not a tax that's ahead of its time - it means the more money you make, the higher percentage of your income you pay in taxes.

Our tax system is divided into chunks called tax brackets. Each bracket has a range of income it applies to and a corresponding tax rate. *Now, here's the part people often get wrong: Moving into a higher tax bracket doesn't mean all your income is taxed at that higher rate. It just means the money you earn within that bracket's range gets taxed at that rate.* The money you earned in the lower bracket? That's still taxed at a lower rate. Pretty fair, right?

Let's break it down with a simple example:

Let's pretend that there are only two tax brackets. For the first bracket, you pay 10% on income up to $10,000. For the second bracket, you pay 20% on any income over $10,000.

Now, let's say you earn $15,000 in a year. Here's how you'd calculate your tax:

1. First, take the money you earned in the first tax bracket, which is $10,000. You pay 10% tax on that, which amounts to $1,000 (10% of $10,000).

2. Next, figure out how much you earned in the second bracket. That's your total income minus the cutoff for the first bracket ($15,000 – $10,000 = $5,000). You pay 20% tax on that, which is $1,000 (20% of $5,000).

3. Add those two amounts together to get your total tax: $1,000 + $1,000 = $2,000.

So, although you moved into a higher tax bracket (the 20% bracket), only the income over $10,000 was taxed at that higher rate. The first $10,000 you earned was still taxed at the lower rate (10%). This is what's meant by our tax system being progressive – as you earn more and move into higher brackets, only the money in those brackets is taxed at the higher rates. The money you earned in lower brackets is taxed at those lower rates. Hope this clears things up!

Credits and Deductions: Your Superheroes in the Tax World

Now that you know about income and tax brackets, let's introduce you to the superheroes of the tax world: tax credits and tax deductions. These guys are your best friends when tax time rolls around because they can seriously shrink your tax bill.

Tax deductions are expenses that you can subtract from your taxable income. Think of it like a discount on the income you're taxed on. Some common deductions include certain education expenses and charitable donations.

Tax credits, on the other hand, are a bit like a gift card that you can use to directly pay off your tax bill. They're even better than deductions because they reduce your taxes dollar for dollar. If you qualify for certain tax credits – like the American Opportunity Tax Credit for education expenses – they can make a huge difference in your final tax bill.

Understanding the basics of income tax might seem daunting at first, but once you get the hang of it, you'll be navigating your tax responsibilities like a pro! It's all part of growing up and becoming financially savvy.

Filing Your First Tax Return

You've likely heard adults in your life grumble about filing their tax returns. But what's the big deal? Simply put, a tax return is how you square up with the government each year. It's your chance to say, "Hey, this is how much I made, here's what I can deduct, and here's what I owe you... or here's what you owe me!" Because, yes, sometimes the government owes you money!

This happens through refunds, which come about if you've paid more in taxes throughout the year than you owe. Picture it like this: you're at a restaurant, you overpay the bill, and your server brings back your change. A tax refund is basically the IRS giving you your change.

The Nuts and Bolts of Tax Filing

So how do you go about filing a tax return? First things first, you need your income information. If you're an employee, that'll be on a form called a W-2 that your employer sends you. If you've done freelance work or gig jobs, you might get a 1099 form instead (or as well).

Then comes the main event: filling out your tax return form. The basic form for this is the 1040. It's like a summary of your financial story for the year.

It's where you list your income, claim any deductions or credits you're eligible for, and calculate how much tax you owe.

Of course, the 1040 isn't the only form you might need. There are extra forms and schedules for specific situations, like if you're claiming certain types of deductions or reporting self-employment income. But don't worry, you'll only need to use the ones that apply to you!

Tax Software and Professionals: Your Trusty Sidekicks

Filing a tax return might sound like navigating a maze, but don't sweat it, you don't have to solve this puzzle on your own. There are plenty of cheat codes and co-players to make the process a breeze. Let's talk about tax software and tax professionals.

Tax software, such as TurboTax, is like your in-game guide that helps you level up through your tax return, one level at a time. It quizzes you about your life (in a non-creepy way), fills in your forms based on your answers, and even calculates the math for you. It's an excellent ally if you're a tech-savvy individual and your tax situation isn't as twisted as a game of Twister.

However, if your situation has more layers than an onion, or you just prefer the reassurance of a human touch, you can recruit a tax professional. These are folks who can speak 'tax' fluently (impressive, right?). They can help you conquer complex tax laws, shrink your tax bill, and ensure your return is as accurate as an archer's arrow.

Whether you prefer the digitized simplicity of software like TurboTax or want to hire a tax whizz, the crucial point is to treat the process like the final boss battle. Give it your best, and aim to ace it.

Tax-Deferred Growth: Your Money's Super Power

Remember 401(k)s and IRAs (from the planning for retirement chapter)? Both 401(k)s and IRAs come with another awesome feature: tax-deferred growth. This means that as your investments earn money, you don't have to pay taxes on those earnings each year. Instead, you pay taxes later when you take the money out. It's a bit like planting a seed and letting it grow into a tree without anyone bothering it. The tree, in this case, is your money, and it can grow bigger and stronger without taxes nibbling at it each year.

If nothing else, the main takeaway from this chapter is that understanding taxes and your paycheck is vital. It's a part of adulting that nobody can escape from, no matter how much we might want to. By understanding this stuff now, you're setting yourself up for success in the future.

Yeah, I know taxes and paychecks can seem dull as dishwater and as complicated as a 1000-piece puzzle, but trust me, you've got this. Keep asking questions, keep learning, and you'll be a tax-savvy superhero in no time. You'll thank yourself later when you can confidently navigate tax season and understand exactly where your hard-earned money is going.

Being a responsible taxpayer isn't just about paying your dues on time, though that is pretty crucial. It's also about knowing why you're paying them, how they're calculated, and how to use the system to your advantage. And who knows, you might even find yourself sparking up a conversation about tax brackets or retirement accounts at your next family gathering!

Your Next Paycheck Challenge

Here's your homework: The next time you get your paycheck, instead of just glancing at the total and tossing it aside, take a closer look. Notice the deductions, see how much is taken out for taxes, and maybe even spot your contributions to your 401(k) or other benefits. It might not be the most thrilling thing in the world, but it's a step toward financial literacy and independence.

Remember, your journey with taxes and paychecks doesn't end here. This is just the beginning. Keep exploring and keep asking questions.

The more knowledge you have, the better decisions you'll be able to make. Speaking of knowledge, are you ready to recall what you've learned in this part about banks, income generation, and taxes?

Ready, Set, Recall

Alright, you've just powered through some pretty key stuff about banks and jobs in the world of finance. Now, it's game time! Let's see how much you've absorbed. Remember, it's totally cool if you don't ace this on the first go. The point is to help you recall and cement what you've learned. If you're curious about the answers, don't worry, they're tucked away in the resources chapter at the back of the book. Ready? Let's roll!

1. What's the main way that banks make their money?
    A) Charging customers for account fees
    B) Selling financial products like insurance
    C) Interest from loans
    D) Offering credit cards

2. What's the difference between a checking and a savings account?
    A) Checking accounts are for spending, savings accounts are for saving
    B) You can only withdraw money from savings accounts once a month
    C) Checking accounts earn more interest
    D) There's no difference; they're just two different names for the same thing

3. What is a Money Market Account?
    A) An account for trading stocks and bonds
    B) A type of savings account that usually requires a higher balance but earns more interest
    C) A bank account for businesses

D) A special account for buying and selling currency

4. What are Certificates of Deposit (CDs)?

A) A type of music storage device

B) Special bank accounts that lock your money for a certain period in exchange for higher interest rates

C) Another name for a checking account

D) A high-interest loan offered by banks

5. Which is an example of active income?

A) Dividends from stocks

B) Rent from a property you own

C) Salary from a job

D) Interest from a savings account

6. What is passive income?

A) Income you earn while sleeping or not actively working

B) The lowest possible income level

C) Income from a part-time job

D) Another name for your salary

7. Which of these could be a source of passive income?

A) Your weekly paycheck

B) Money earned from a garage sale

C) Earnings from a blog or YouTube channel that you monetize

D) Winning a cash prize

8. How does your career choice affect your income potential?

A) Different careers have different average income levels

B) Your career choice doesn't affect your income

C) Certain careers prevent you from earning passive income

D) You can only earn active income if you work in a high-paying career

9. Why are interest rates important in banking?

   A) They determine how much money you can borrow

   B) They influence the amount of money you earn or pay in interest

   C) They control the number of bank accounts you can open

   D) They are the same as inflation rates

10. What role does technology play in income generation in the digital age?

   A) Technology has opened up new opportunities to earn income, such as blogging or vlogging

   B) Technology has made it harder to earn income

   C) Technology has no influence on income generation

   D) Technology has made traditional jobs obsolete

11. What are income taxes

   a) The money you owe to your state for living there.

   b) The money you owe to charities.

   c) The money you owe to the government based on your income.

   d) The money you owe to your employer.

12. What is a paycheck breakdown?

   a) A list of reasons why you're paid less than your colleagues.

   b) A detailed explanation of what your pay consists of, including gross pay, net pay, and any deductions.

   c) A list of ways you can spend your paycheck.

   d) A chart showing how your pay has decreased over time.

13. Why might someone need a financial advisor for tax purposes?

   a) To get a loan for tax payments.

   b) To explain complex tax laws and help with filing tax returns.

   c) To lower their tax bracket.

   d) To donate their taxes to charities.

14. What is a common document required for filing a tax return?

a) A W-2 form

b) A grocery receipt

c) A charitable giving receipt

d) A rent receipt

15. What happens if you fail to file a tax return or file it late?

   a) You might face penalties or interest charges from the IRS.

   b) You will receive a refund from the government.

   c) Your employer will withhold future paychecks.

   d) Nothing, it's optional to file a tax return.

16. What is social responsibility in terms of finance?

   a) Investing only in socially responsible companies.

   b) Giving a part of your income to the government.

   c) Being mindful of how your financial decisions affect society.

   d) Keeping all your money to yourself.

17. What's a primary reason for understanding your paycheck?

   a) To negotiate your salary.

   b) To ensure you're being paid accurately and understand deductions.

   c) To figure out how much to spend on entertainment.

   d) To compare with your colleagues' paychecks.

III

Part 3 - The Financial Fitness Regime: Budgets, Spending, and Savings

Chapter 7 - Budgeting: A Money Management Essential

Why Budgeting is Your Superpower?

A lright, so we've all heard the term "budget", right? It gets tossed around like a frisbee on a sunny day. But have you ever really paused to think about what it means and why it's actually a super essential tool to have in your arsenal? Hold on tight, because we're about to demystify it.

Picture this: You've been eyeing that latest smartphone, but your savings jar isn't exactly brimming with spare change. Major letdown, right? But what if I told you there's a secret weapon that could help you nab that dream phone without breaking the bank? And you know who wields that weapon? It's you, with the might of budgeting at your side!

Think of a budget as your financial GPS - guiding you towards your money goals - be it that swanky phone, the newest gaming console, or that epic road trip with your buddies. It's all about understanding where your cash is rolling in from (Is it your weekly pocket money? A part-time gig?) and where it's rolling out to (Streaming movies? Snagging the latest graphic novels? Stashing away for college?).

By setting a budget, you're becoming the boss of your bucks, instead of letting them boss you around. It's like you're the pilot of your own financial airplane, navigating it towards your money dreams and away from the stormy weather of overspending.

Budgeting IRL: Here's the Proof

You might be asking, "Alright, this sounds pretty neat, but does budgeting really work?" Well, how about a couple of real-life stories to make you a true convert?

Let's talk about Mia. At 18, she's a total fashion fiend. She used to spend her entire part-time paycheck on the latest trends, only to scramble to cover her other bills. But then she discovered budgeting, and you know what? She's still shopping, but she's also saving for her dream to study fashion design in college.

And then there's Lucas, the gamer. A few years back, Lucas was in a bind when the newest gaming console hit the market. His wallet was running empty, and he just couldn't afford it. But once he embraced budgeting, not only did he score that console, but he also started saving for a game development course.

Both Mia and Lucas aren't financial wizards. They simply mastered the art of budgeting. And the coolest part is, you can do the same! So, are you ready to take a deep dive into the world of budgeting?

A DIY Guide to Your First Budge

It's time for you to dive into the world of budgeting. Together, we're going to navigate the path to your very first budget. We'll figure out your financial aspirations, pinpoint your sources of income, and list all those sneaky bills and expenses. Plus, we'll add practical examples and sprinkle in helpful tips to enrich your budgeting journey. Let's get started!

Step 1: Identify Your Financial Goals

First and foremost, let's talk dreams. What are you squirreling away your pennies for? Eyeing the latest smartphone model? Or maybe you're hoarding funds for a killer road trip with friends? From small splurges to major expenditures, each goal is important. Identifying your goals not only makes budgeting more meaningful but also motivational. Remember, these aren't just arbitrary numbers - they're stepping stones to your dreams!

Tip: Be specific with your goals and give them a timeframe. Instead of "save for a new phone," aim for "save $700 for a new phone by December." This gives you a clear target and helps you measure your progress. We'll dive deeper into financial goal setting in chapter 14, so stay tuned!

Step 2: Determine Your Income

Now let's turn our attention to what's coming in each month. This could stem from a variety of sources: your part-time job, weekly allowance, or even that creative Etsy shop you manage in your free time. Don't leave anything out - even the small streams can add up to a substantial river!

For example, let's say you make $150 per month from your part-time job at the local bookstore, receive $50 a week as an allowance, and make around $100 a month from your Etsy shop. That adds up to a monthly income of $450.

Step 3: List Your Regular Expenses

Time to face the inevitable - your expenses. This includes everything from that irresistible weekly burger to the subscription services you're signed up for, and of course, the money you're setting aside for your financial goals. Be as thorough as you can - tracking every dollar can offer surprising insights into your spending habits.

Practical Tip: Use an app or a spreadsheet to categorize and track your expenses. This will provide you with a visual representation of where your money goes and can help identify areas where you might be overspending.

As we wrap up these steps, remember that a budget isn't set in stone - it's a living, breathing plan that adapts to your changing circumstances and priorities. So don't worry if your first budget isn't perfect; what matters is that you've taken the first crucial step towards financial independence. Keep refining and adjusting as you go, and you'll be mastering the art of budgeting in no time!

Tracking Your Budget Like a Pro

Let's get real. You've put all this work into creating your budget, but it's only going to do its thing if you keep a keen eye on it. Let's dive into how you can do just that, without it feeling like another chore.

Keep it Classic: The Receipt Collecting Method

Old school? Yes. Effective? Absolutely. Simply start keeping all your receipts and at the end of the week (or day if you're super keen), go through them and tally up how much you've spent. Make it a ritual. Get yourself a snack, put on some music, and make it a money moment. The best part about this method? It's great for visual learners who like to physically see where their money is going.

Get Your Spreadsheet On

If you're a fan of numbers and tables, then this method might be your jam.

Create a spreadsheet with categories of all your expenses. As you spend, update your spreadsheet. It might seem a bit time-consuming at first, but once you get the hang of it, it'll be a breeze. Plus, it's a great skill to have for future life and work.

Embrace the Tech: Budgeting Apps

For those of you who live in the digital world, budgeting apps can be your best friend. Apps like Mint, PocketGuard, or You Need a Budget (YNAB) can connect to your bank account and automatically track your income and expenses. Be sure to check out the resources section to check out the budgeting apps we love to use ourselves!

They give you a real-time snapshot of your spending habits, and some even send notifications if you're nearing your budget limit. Super handy, right?

Set Regular Check-ins

Regardless of the method you choose, it's crucial to set regular check-ins with your budget. Maybe it's every Friday afternoon or the first of the month—whatever works for you. Regular check-ins will help you see if you're on track with your budget or if there are areas you need to adjust.

Remember, tracking your budget isn't about restricting your fun; it's about making sure you have the money to have even more fun in the future! So, stay on top of it and watch your financial goals get closer each day.

Tuning Your Budget to Your Life's Rhythm

Just like your favorite playlist, sometimes your budget needs a little tuning. Life can hit you with surprises—maybe you scored a new part-time job, or you've decided to join a gym, or your best friend's birthday is coming up. In these times, your budget needs to change gears and adapt. Here's how you can do it like a pro.

Responding to Income Changes

Let's say you've just landed a new gig that pays more (woohoo!). That's awesome, but it also means it's time to adjust your budget. You could allocate some of this extra cash to your savings, or maybe splurge a little on something you've had your eye on. On the flip side, if your income decreases, you'll need to cut back on some of your spending. It's not the most fun, but it'll keep your finances healthy.

Adjusting for Lifestyle Changes

Started hitting the gym? Got into a new hobby that costs a bit more than you thought? Life changes and your budget should too. Take a look at your expenses and see where you can make room for these new costs. It could mean spending less on eating out, or maybe you decide to cut back on streaming services.

Planning for Special Occasions

We all know that feeling when a friend's birthday creeps up out of nowhere. Or maybe it's the holiday season, and you want to buy gifts for your loved ones. These are the perfect times to tweak your budget. You can start by setting aside a little extra cash in the months leading up to these events.

Handling Unexpected Expenses

Life can throw some curveballs like your bike needing a sudden repair or your phone screen cracking. These unexpected expenses can throw your budget off balance if you're not prepared. It's a good idea to have an emergency funds section in your budget for these just-in-case moments. Don't worry we'll talk more about how to set up this emergency fund in Chapter 8.

Remember, your budget is not a prison, but more of a guide. It's there to help you, not limit you. As your life changes, your budget should too. So, don't stress about making adjustments. After all, it's all part of becoming a budgeting pro!

Case Study: Navigating Unpredictable Financial Waters

To show you the magic of a rainy-day fund, let's dive into a real-life story. Let's talk about Ben.

Ben is a high school sophomore who loves photography. He saved up for months to buy a used professional camera to enhance his skills. Once he bought the camera, he started setting aside a few dollars every week into a rainy-day fund, just in case something went wrong with his beloved camera.

A few months later, his camera started acting up and needed a repair that would cost a fair chunk of cash. Now, if Ben didn't have his rainy-day fund, he might have had to sacrifice something else he loved, like his weekend movie nights or his comic book collection.

But guess what? Ben's rainy-day fund came to the rescue. He was able to pay for the camera repair without giving up his other passions. All because he had the foresight to plan for unexpected expenses in his budget.

Just like Ben, you can make your budget your ally against the unexpected. By being prepared for irregular expenses, you're not only taking charge of your financial journey, but you're also keeping the stress of surprise costs at bay. Now that's what I call a win-win!

And there you have it, folks! The fantastic world of budgeting, explained. Whether it's saving for a hot new gadget or keeping a cushion for those not-so-great unexpected costs, budgeting is your secret weapon in the world of personal finance. It's more than just crunching numbers. It's about empowering yourself to make confident financial decisions that fit your life and your goals.

Remember, a budget isn't a limitation. Instead, it's a financial roadmap that helps you make the most out of your money while keeping your spending habits in check. It's about understanding where your money goes and making conscious decisions about how to spend it.

Now that we've got a grip on budgeting, it's time to step onto the next stage of our money journey. Are you ready to delve into the art of spending wisely? Up next, we'll tackle how to make your money stretch further, find better deals, and avoid those pesky pitfalls that can empty our pockets faster than we'd like. Stay tuned, because Chapter 7 is all about becoming a smart spender and making your hard-earned cash work for you.

Chapter 8 - Spending Wisely

Understanding the Difference Between Wants and Needs

F irst up on our journey is figuring out the difference between wants and needs. It may seem like we're heading back to school, but trust me, nailing this can totally flip your spending game.

Needs are the absolute must-haves. The essentials. The things you can't survive without. Think food, a place to live, clothes on your back, or healthcare. Then you've got wants - things that are super cool to have, but your life isn't hanging in the balance if you don't. Those slick designer jeans, the newest smartphone, or the trendy sneakers you've been ogling? All wants.

Why should you care? Well, understanding what's a need and what's a want can help you prioritize your spending, keep your cash flow steady, and avoid financial headaches. By focusing on your needs first, you can make sure your basics are covered before splurging on your wants.

Unmasking Your Wants and Needs

Alright, so how do you go about figuring out your personal needs and wants? It can be a bit tricky because sometimes things feel like they're needs when they're actually wants.

Here's a handy tool: When you're thinking about buying something, ask yourself, "Do I need this to survive or would it just be nice to have?" *Remember, it's totally okay to have wants. But when it comes to managing your budget, your needs should be sitting in the driver's seat.*

Wants vs. Needs: Picture This

To help you get a grip on this, let's throw in some examples:

1. You're feeling peckish and need to eat. Food is the need here. But what about that pizza you're craving? That's a want. You need food, but you want pizza.

2. You need a phone to stay connected with your people, but do you need the latest and greatest model? Probably not. That's a want. A working phone, though, that's a need.

3. Sure, you need clothes to wear, but does it have to be designer gear? Nah, that's a want. Just some decent threads to cover you up is the need.

Getting the hang of it? By knowing your wants from your needs, you're setting yourself up for some seriously smart spending. And who doesn't want that, right?

Now when you do buy things you want, doing price comparisons before you buy could virtually make or break your budget.

Shop Like Sherlock: The How-To of Price Comparisons

Imagine you've been eyeing this totally cool skateboard online. You're ready to hit "Buy Now", but a little voice tells you to pause. It could be your inner Sherlock Holmes hinting there might be a better deal somewhere else. That's the essence of comparison shopping!

Comparison shopping is like conducting a mini-investigation. You're hunting for the best prices across different stores and online platforms for the same item. And believe it or not, it's not as tough as it sounds. The internet is your magnifying glass - a quick search or a visit to a price comparison site and boom, you're comparing prices like a pro.

Why do this, you ask? Well, prices can be a bit of a wild card. They change from place to place. By doing a smidge of research, you might snag a killer deal and save some of your well-deserved cash.

The Battle of Quality vs Quantity: Unmasking the Real Value

Let's dive into another essential element of spending wisely: the ultimate showdown of Quality vs Quantity. You've probably heard, "You get what you pay for," and that can be super true. At times, going for the pricier option can be a smarter choice in the long run.

Picture this: you're on the hunt for a new backpack. You could grab the cheapest one, but if it rips apart after a few months, you'll have to shell out for another. But if you go for a slightly pricier, sturdier backpack, it might stick with you for years. In the end, you save cash and the trouble of repeat backpack-hunting trips!

So, it's not just about the price tag. It's about the value you're getting for your money. Will it last? Is it a better performer? These are some questions you should ask yourself before you make a purchase.

Dollars that Stretch: Unleash the Power of Smart Shopping

Alright, you're now a pro at price comparisons and assessing quality. Ready for more tips to make your dollars do the splits?

Here's the scoop:

- **The clock is ticking:** Sales often pop up at specific times - end of a season, after holidays, etc. Having an eye on the calendar can get you some cool deals.

- **Coupons and discounts:** They're your best pals! There are tons of apps out there that can give you a heads-up about discounts.

- **The lure of sales tactics:** Stores have their tricks to get you to spend. Ever heard of "Limited time offer!" or "Buy one, get one half off!"? They're all strategies to pull you in. Keep a cool head, don't get carried away by the excitement, and stick to your budget.

Being a smart spender isn't just about cutting corners and saving. It's about making every dollar count. With these nifty tricks in your pocket, you're all set to get the most out of your hard-earned cash!

The Reality of Instant Gratification

Ever had a sudden urge to buy that stylish new pair of sneakers, even though your closet is already bursting with them? That, my friend, is instant gratification at play! It's a psychological phenomenon that pushes us to seek immediate pleasure or reward, skipping over any potential long-term benefits or consequences.

Let's make this clear with an example. You're scrolling through your social media feed and *bam!* there's an ad for the latest smartphone, even though you just got a new one a few months ago. But that's not important because you want this shiny new thing, right now! That's instant gratification nudging you to impulse buy.

Unmasking the Wizards: The Influence of Marketing and Advertising

You might think you're immune to the tricks of the marketing world, but guess what? We all get influenced! Companies know exactly how to tap into our desire for instant gratification. Clever advertising can make us feel like we absolutely need that new product right this minute. How could we even breathe without it?

And with digital platforms, this has skyrocketed. Ads are literally at our fingertips. Picture-perfect influencers endorsing products, flashy banners announcing "limited period" sales, or those sneaky notifications about items in our wish list going out of stock — it's all a grand scheme to make us spend more, and more often.

Leveling Up Your Game: Resisting the Siren Call of Instant Gratification

It's not an epic battle against a supervillain, but you can totally suit up with these strategies to tame the beast of instant gratification.

First up, *mindful spending*. Instead of reaching for your wallet at the sight of a 'new arrival', take a moment. Do you genuinely need this item? Is it adding value to your life, or just satisfying a short-lived craving?

Another cool hack is setting a waiting period for purchases. If you're eyeing a pricey item, don't rush. Set a waiting period — say, 48 hours or a week. If you still want it after cooling off, it might be a worthy purchase.

Lastly, structure your budget. Having a clear financial plan gives you a sense of where your money is going and how much you can afford to spend on non-essentials.

Remember, it's about progress, not perfection. So even if you falter once or twice, don't beat yourself up. Becoming a wise spender is a journey, and you're on the right path!

The Tale of a Prudent Spender

Let's zoom into the real-world story of Jenna, a high school junior with a serious love for fashion. Jenna was known for her unique style, but her passion was leaving her wallet painfully thin. Each time her favorite online stores launched a new collection or she passed by her beloved local boutiques, the urge to splurge was tough to resist.

Jenna knew this couldn't continue, especially with college just around the corner. So, she decided to make a change. She started distinguishing her wants from her needs, a vital step towards a healthier financial situation. She made a list of essential clothing items she genuinely needed and discovered that her "wants" far outnumbered her "needs".

Armed with this revelation, Jenna then turned her attention towards shopping smartly. Instead of blindly buying the first item that caught her eye, she started comparing prices across different online stores and physical boutiques. She subscribed to newsletters, kept an eye out for sales, and discovered the thrill of hunting for the best deal. It was almost like a game to her, where the prize was savings!

Jenna also began realizing the power of quality over quantity. Instead of going for the cheaper alternatives that didn't last long, she started investing in higher-priced items that were durable and timeless. It cost more upfront, but she saved money in the long run as she didn't need to replace these items often.

The biggest challenge, however, was wrestling with the beast of instant gratification. To combat this, Jenna created a rule for herself. If an item wasn't on her "needs" list, she would wait for at least a week before deciding whether to buy it. This waiting period allowed her to evaluate whether she genuinely wanted the item or if it was just a fleeting desire.

And guess what? These changes started making a massive difference. Jenna noticed that she was saving more money than ever before. She could now afford to contribute to her college fund, without compromising her passion for fashion.

Jenna's story shows us that it's entirely possible to balance our desires and our financial well-being. With a dash of self-awareness, a sprinkle of smart shopping, and a big scoop of patience, we can be in control of our spending and, ultimately, our financial future.

There you have it! Spending wisely isn't about denying yourself of all fun and desires, it's about making smarter choices that will positively impact your finances and future. It's all about balance - indulging in your passions without going overboard, and managing your money so that it aligns with your short-term wants and long-term needs.

And remember, the path to becoming a savvy spender isn't a sprint; it's a marathon. It's a journey that demands time, patience, and lots of practice. But don't worry - as you traverse this path, you'll gain a deeper understanding of your spending habits and make more informed decisions. You'll learn how to navigate the financial landscape with grace and confidence.

So, now that we've navigated the twists and turns of spending wisely, it's time to take a giant leap into our next big topic - saving. You might be thinking, "Wait, didn't we just talk about spending?" Well, yes, we did. But guess what? Spending and saving are two sides of the same coin. One fuels the other, and together, they create a balanced financial equation.

In the upcoming chapter, we'll dive into the why's and how's of saving, explore the magic of compound interest, and understand how saving can help us reach our financial goals faster. If you're ready to kickstart your savings journey and transform your financial future, buckle up!

Chapter 9 - The Importance of Saving

Alright, get ready for a plot twist. We're not here to talk about making a fast buck or discovering some secret trick to morph into an overnight millionaire. Instead, we're gonna chat about something you're familiar with but might not have really thought about in the grand scheme of things – yeah, it's saving money.

Now, don't get me wrong. Saving isn't about squirreling away your money under your mattress and forgetting about it. It's way more powerful than that. Saving is about letting your cash do some of the heavy lifting, ensuring you're ready for whatever life throws at you, and, here's the real kicker, helping you break free and stand tall in your financial journey. But how does this all come together? Hold onto that thought. We'll get there.

The Superpower Called Saving

You might be thinking, "Why bother saving? I could be living it up, buying stuff I want right now!" And I get it. Why stash your cash away when you could be enjoying the fruits of your labor right now? But here's the deal: saving money is all about being future savvy. It's making sure your future self isn't left out in the cold and can handle whatever surprises come down the track.

When you save, you're building a financial buffer zone. Got a sudden expense? No sweat, you've got savings. Want to snag something pricey without sinking into debt? Boom, your savings have got your back. Craving a slice of financial independence where you're not forever stressing about dough? You've hit the nail on the head - saving is your golden ticket.

The Power of Starting Early

Okay, let's kick things off by answering a straightforward question. When do you think is the best time to start saving? Should you wait until you're raking in some serious cash with a full-time job? Or can you start when you're still in your teens, working a part-time gig, or getting an allowance? *Here's the golden rule of saving: the sooner, the better.*

The Cool Perks of Starting Early

First off, let's make one thing clear. Saving isn't just about hoarding every penny and living like a miser. Nah, it's about learning to manage your money and not letting it manage you. Starting to save early gives you a head start in the race to financial discipline. You learn to control your spending, separate your wants from your needs, and, most importantly, understand that instant gratification isn't always the best path.

And here's the biggie - starting to save early gives your money more time to grow. Yeah, you heard that right. Your money can grow, all thanks to a neat thing called compound interest. We'll dig deeper into that magical concept later. But for now, just know that the longer you keep your money saved, the more it multiplies. It's like having a magic money tree!

Storytime: Unveiling the Magic of Early Saving

Now, let's spice things up with a little story. Meet Sam and Alex, both dreaming of buying their dream car by the age of 30. Sam starts saving $100 a month at 18, while Alex waits until they're 25 to start saving the same amount.

By the time they hit 30, Sam would've saved $14,400, and Alex would've saved only $6,000. But wait, there's more! If they'd stashed their savings in a savings account with a 2% interest rate, Sam would end up with about $16,386 thanks to compound interest. Alex, on the other hand, would only have about $6,365. So, who gets to drive off with their dream car? Yup, it's our early bird, Sam!

Now, your mileage may vary. You might not be able to save $100 each month, and that's okay. ***The key takeaway here isn't about the amount. It's about the habit and the timing.*** Even saving a small amount consistently can lead to big rewards over time.

Just remember, starting early isn't about depriving yourself of all fun and living a penny-pinching life. It's about being smart with your money, setting yourself up for a stress-free future, and yeah, possibly even snagging that dream car someday! So, why wait? Time's ticking, and the sooner you get your savings game on, the brighter your financial future could be.

What's This Thing Called Compound Interest?

Money multiplying itself? Sounds like some kind of wizardry, doesn't it? But no, it's just the fantastic world of compound interest. It's like your money has superpowers, growing over time. So let's dive in and unmask the superhero of the savings world, shall we?

Decoding Compound Interest: It's Simpler Than You Think

Here's how to picture compound interest - it's like your money having babies. And then those babies have babies. Weird? Maybe a bit. But it makes sense, promise!

Let's say you save $100 in a bank account that gives you 5% interest per year. After one year, you'd have $105. That's your original hundred bucks, plus five more - that's the interest you earned.

But here's where it gets interesting. In the second year, you're not just earning 5% on your original $100. You're also earning 5% on the extra $5 you got in the first year. So, at the end of year two, you're looking at about $110.25. Those quarters may seem like small change now, but give it some time, and you'll start to see it stack up!

Why Compound Interest Loves Long-term Savings

Okay, so you've got the basics. Now, why should you care? Well, compound interest is like the secret weapon for your long-term savings. The trick is to give it time to work its magic.

Imagine planting a seed and then pulling it out of the ground every few days to check if it's grown. It's never going to turn into a tree, right? But if you plant it and leave it there, taking care of it, over time, it will grow into a strong, sturdy tree.

That's exactly how your savings work. The longer you let your money sit and earn compound interest, the more it will grow. Yes, it may start slow, but just like that tiny seed, given time, it can become a towering tree.

So, feeling excited? You should be! That's the wonder of compound interest. It's not about overnight riches, but understanding how to make your money work for you.

Short-term vs. Long-term Saving Goals: What's the Deal?

Okay, time to chat about something super important: your goals. We all have things we're itching to buy or do, right? So, how do we turn those dreamy wants into something more...well, real? This is where short-term and long-term saving goals enter the scene.

Short-term and Long-term Goals: What's the Difference?

So, short-term and long-term goals are like your little and big dreams. Simple, right?

Short-term goals are the stuff you want to snag pretty soon—think in the next year or so. Maybe it's a slick pair of kicks you've been eyeballing or saving up for that concert with your squad. They're like immediate gratification goodies.

Long-term goals, though, are the dreams you're gunning for in the future. Stuff like saving up for college, buying a car, or even starting your own business someday. Yup, these are the big-ticket items.

How to Juggle Saving for Short-term and Long-term Goals

Alright, so how do you manage to save for short-term and long-term goals without your brain going into meltdown mode? Well, it's all about balance and knowing what's up on your priority list.

For the short-term stuff, think about setting up a savings account and dropping a set amount into it each month. Even if it's just a couple of dollars, it's still progress! Trust me, you'll be surprised how quickly it all adds up.

As for those long-term goals, remember our buddy compound interest? Yeah, this is where that bad boy comes into play. Remember, compound interest is all about the long game. The more time you give your money to grow, the more dough you'll rake in from interest. So, start putting a little bit away into a long-term savings account or maybe even a Certificate of Deposit (CD) which tends to offer higher interest rates.

Now, I know what you're thinking: "But I've got more goals than cash!" I get it. When income is tight and you've got multiple dreams on the horizon, it's all about figuring out what's most important to you right now. Then, divvy up your savings accordingly. It's totally okay to save a bit less for your long-term goal if you're super stoked about a short-term one, and vice versa.

Remember, stashing away money, whether for short-term or long-term goals, is about building a secure future for yourself. Each cent you save is getting you one step closer to making your dreams a reality.

What's an Emergency Fund?

Buckle up, because we're about to get real. Life can sometimes be a box of chocolates, and not always the sweet kind. Sometimes, it throws us those unexpected sour lemon ones that we weren't ready for, and it's our job to deal with them. In the world of money, these are the unexpected expenses, and that's where the knight in shining armor comes in—enter the emergency fund.

The Why Behind an Emergency Fund

First, let's answer this: what's an emergency fund? Well, it's kinda like a safety net or a cushion. It's money you've stashed away to cover life's not-so-fun surprises. Think unexpected car repairs, medical emergencies, or even losing a job.

Why should you care? Well, having an emergency fund can keep you from dipping into your savings or worse, racking up debt. It's all about being prepared and giving yourself peace of mind. Because who wants to be stressing about cash when you're already dealing with an unexpected setback?

Your Guide to Building an Emergency Fund

So, how big should this safety cushion be? Well, most money wizards suggest having three to six months' worth of living expenses stashed away. I know it sounds like a lot, but it's not something you have to pull together overnight.

Start small. Even if it's just saving a few dollars from each paycheck or putting aside any extra cash from birthdays or part-time jobs. You could even open a dedicated savings account for your emergency fund. This way, you won't be tempted to use it for non-emergency things (like that tempting sale at your favorite store).

And guess what? Your emergency fund isn't set in stone. As your life changes, your emergency fund should grow with you. Moving out and taking on more bills? Your emergency fund should increase to match.

Remember, an emergency fund isn't about being a downer—it's about being ready. It's not saying "bad things will happen," but rather "if bad things happen, I've got this!" And the peace of mind that comes with that? Well, that's priceless.

Figuring Out Your Perfect Saving Amount

So, we've been chatting about saving, but you might be wondering, "How much should I actually be saving?" Well, my friend, that's a pretty solid question and we're about to dive into it. Saving is like picking out your favorite outfit - it's personal and it's got to fit just right. So let's play financial stylist and find your money sweet spot!

Crafting Your Custom Saving Plan

There's no one-size-fits-all answer to how much you should save because everyone's situation is unique. But a pretty popular rule of thumb is the 50/30/20 rule. It's like the Golden Ratio of personal finance. Here's how it breaks down:

- 50% of your income goes to necessities (think: food, housing, bills).
- 30% is for wants (yeah, that includes the new kicks you've been eyeing).
- 20% goes straight to savings.

But remember, this is just a guideline. If you're saving for something big, or you want to build your emergency fund quicker, you might decide to stash away more than 20%. On the flip side, if you're just starting to save and 20% seems like a massive mountain, start with a smaller percentage and work your way up. The key is to find a balance that works for you and stick to it.

Staying Flexible: Your Saving Habits Aren't Set in Stone

One thing to remember - your saving habits should flex with your life. Got a raise at work? Awesome! Consider boosting your savings rate. Unexpected expenses threw a curveball at you? It's okay to dial back your savings for a bit until you get back on track.

And check in on your saving habits regularly. Maybe once every few months, sit down and have a heart-to-heart with your finances. Are you saving enough? Too much? Could you do better? Just like you grow and evolve, so should your saving habits.

Remember, it's not just about the dollars you save, but about building a habit of saving. So be patient with yourself, adjust when needed, and celebrate your progress. After all, every buck you save is one step closer to your goals!

Fun and Effective Saving Strategies" - Level Up Your Savings Game

So, you've stuck around this far, meaning you're seriously interested in this whole saving thing, right? But let's face it, saving isn't always the most thrilling part of your day. Well, until now, that is. Let's flip the script and turn saving from a dull task into an exciting game. Are you ready to level up your savings game?

Taking on the Savings Challenge

Think of savings like your favorite sport or video game, only this time, you're racking up dollars instead of points. Ever heard of the '52-Week Money Challenge'? You start by saving $1 in the first week, then $2 in the second week, and so on, until you're saving $52 in the last week. That might sound intense, but by the end of the year, you'll have an impressive $1,378 saved up!

If that seems too hardcore, don't stress. You can modify the challenge to suit you. Start by saving a dime a day and then add a dime each week. By the end of the year, you'll have a tidy sum saved up.

Round Up the Change and Go Auto

Next, let's talk about the 'round-up rule'. With this nifty trick, your bank rounds up your purchases to the nearest dollar and puts the difference in your savings account. It's like discovering hidden treasure in your own bank account!

And how about going auto? Most banks allow you to set up automatic transfers from your checking to your savings account. It's like having a little savings elf quietly moving your cash around in the background. Before you know it, you'll have a growing stash of savings.

Find Your Groove

The goal here is to make saving fun and exciting. Experiment with different strategies, mix them up, or even come up with your own. The best strategy will make you look forward to saving and keep you motivated to reach your goals. Remember, there's no one-size-fits-all when it comes to saving. You do you.

So, are you ready to make saving a fun part of your day? With the right strategy, you'll be a savings champ in no time!

The Role of Saving in Budgeting - Where Saving Fits in Your Money Masterplan

So, we've been talking a lot about saving, right? But where exactly does saving fit into the bigger picture, that grand tapestry we call a budget? Well, strap in, my financially savvy friends, because we're about to unravel that mystery.

Saving: The Superstar of Your Budget

First up, let's get this straight: saving isn't just some random bystander in your budget; it's a superstar player. Yeah, you heard it right. Saving takes center stage when you're mapping out your financial roadmap.

Here's the thing: a budget is like a pie, and each slice represents a part of your money - rent, food, phone bills, weekend fun, and yep, savings. Without a saving slice, your pie isn't complete. Not convinced? Well, imagine this: you're going about your day, and boom, your laptop gives up on you. Now, if you've been feeding your savings slice, you'll have the money to replace it without freaking out or maxing out a credit card. That's why savings is so darn important.

Making Saving a Regular Thing

Now, how do we make saving a regular part of the budgeting routine? Well, it's all about giving savings the VIP treatment it deserves.

Here's a top-notch tip: don't just save what's left after spending; spend what's left after saving. Mind-blowing, right? The moment your cash lands in your account, set aside your saving slice right away. You can even set up automatic transfers to your savings account so you won't forget or be tempted to skip it.

And remember that saving amount we figured out in the last section? Stick to it. Consistency is key. As your income grows or your expenses change, don't forget to revisit your saving amount and adjust it accordingly. Keep that savings slice juicy and growing.

To sum it all up, saving is the silent hero in your budget. It keeps you covered for those rainy days and big dreams. So, don't sideline it. Instead, give it the spotlight it deserves, and you'll be amazed at how it transforms your budgeting game. And who knows, with savings as your trusty sidekick, you might just end up being the superhero of your own financial story.

How Saving Can Create Financial Independence

Alright, we're diving into the deep end of why we're doing all this saving stuff in the first place. Yep, we're talking about financial independence. It sounds like a big, fancy term, but it's actually something pretty simple and pretty awesome.

Building a Fortress with Your Savings

You see, financial independence is all about having enough money stashed away so that you can make your own choices. It's like building a fortress where you're the boss, and you decide what goes in and what comes out.

Let's get real for a sec. You know those chores you hate doing, but you have to do because, well, you need your allowance? Imagine a world where you don't have to do that anymore because you've got enough saved up to fund your lifestyle. That's financial independence.

And guess what? Your savings are the building blocks of that fortress. Every time you tuck some money away, you're adding a brick to your financial fortress. And the more bricks you add, the stronger your fortress gets, protecting you from unexpected expenses and giving you the freedom to do what you want. That's the real power of saving, my friends.

Visualizing Your Financial Future

Now, here's where things get super exciting. I want you to close your eyes and picture your life in the future. You've been consistently saving and your fortress is strong and tall. What does it look like?

Are you sipping coconut water on a beach somewhere, free from the 9 to 5 grind? Or maybe you're running your own business, doing something you love? Or perhaps you're living in a city apartment, pursuing a career that sets your heart on fire?

That's your future financial independence. It might seem a bit far-off now, but remember: every saving step you take now brings you closer to that dream.

And hey, don't just dream about it. Set your saving goals to make it happen. How much would you need to save to make that beach bum life a reality? Or to start that business? Or move to that city?

Set those goals, break them down into smaller steps, and then smash them one by one.

So there you have it. Saving isn't just about hoarding pennies. It's about building a future where you're in control. A future where you're financially independent. And trust me, there's nothing quite like the feeling of knowing you've built that all by yourself. Keep saving, keep building, and you'll get there. Promise.

Just remember that saving is about making small, consistent steps toward your financial goals. And with each step, you're building a future where you're in control.

So, here's my challenge to you: Start today. Even if it's just a tiny step, it's a step in the right direction. And before you know it, you'll look back and see how far you've come.

Remember, your future financial independence is worth every penny you save today. So, here's to you and your savings journey. You've got this!

Ready to see if you remember what you've learned in part 3 of the book? Flip over and answer the quiz!

Ready, Set, Recall

Alright, buckle up and let's see how much you've taken in from the rollercoaster ride that was Part 3 - Budgeting, Spending, and Saving! This is just a fun way to recap the concepts and ideas we've covered. Don't stress if you miss a question or two. This is just to help you reflect on your learning journey. Remember, the answer key can be found at the back of the book in the resources chapter.

1. What's the main purpose of budgeting?
    a) To stop you from spending money
    b) To make you feel guilty about your spending habits
    c) To help you manage your money and plan for the future
    d) To make sure you never buy anything fun

2. What's the difference between a 'want' and a 'need'?
    a) They're the same thing
    b) A 'need' is something you can't live without, a 'want' is something you would like to have
    c) A 'want' is something you can't live without, a 'need' is something you would like to have
    d) There's no difference, it's just a matter of opinion

3. Why should you start saving early?
    a) Because it's easier to save when you're young
    b) Because of compound interest

c) Because your parents told you to

d) Because it's a fun hobby

4. What is an emergency fund?

a) Money set aside for unexpected expenses

b) Money saved for your next holiday

c) Money set aside for a new phone

d) Money saved for your weekly grocery shopping

5. What is the role of saving in budgeting?

a) Saving is not related to budgeting

b) Saving allows you to purchase everything you want

c) Saving contributes to your financial plan and helps you reach your financial goals

d) Saving is only for people who earn a lot of money

6. Why is it important to differentiate between short-term and long-term saving goals?

a) It's not important

b) It helps you plan and prioritize your savings

c) Short-term goals are more important than long-term goals

d) Long-term goals are more important than short-term goals

7. What is meant by instant gratification?

a) Saving money for the future

b) The desire to experience pleasure or fulfillment without delay or defer-ment

c) The pleasure one gets from saving money

d) The satisfaction of buying things on sale

8. What is a prudent spender?

a) Someone who never spends money

b) Someone who spends without thinking

c) Someone who makes thoughtful decisions about their spending

d) Someone who always buys the most expensive items

9. Which of these is NOT a good practice for tracking your budget?

a) Reviewing your budget daily

b) Ignoring small expenses

c) Keeping receipts and recording expenses

d) Using a budgeting app

10. Why can compound interest be a powerful tool for saving?

a) Because it's difficult to calculate

b) Because it allows your money to grow exponentially over time

c) Because it makes your bank account look good

d) Because it's a fancy financial term

IV

Part 4 - The Borrower's Handbook: Mastering Credit and Loans

Chapter 10 - Borrowing and Debt - A Survival Guide

Okay, so what exactly does it mean to borrow? Imagine you're eyeing this super cool gadget but your wallet's telling you, "Not today, bud." So you reach out to your bank, a lending company, or maybe even a buddy, and say, "Mind if I owe you?" Basically, borrowing means getting some money now with a solid promise that you'll repay it down the line. But remember, this isn't free cash. It's like a loaner sweatshirt—you've gotta give it back.

Debunking Debt

Alright, onto debt. You've asked for money and got it. But that cash you borrowed? You're obliged to repay it. That's what we call debt. But hang on, there's more. This thing called debt brings along a few friends—principal, interest, and repayment schedule.

The principal is just the amount you borrowed initially. Not too tricky, right? Interest, however, is like the rent you pay for using someone else's money. It's a bit extra on top of the principal that the lender charges. So, the more time you take to repay, the more you'll end up paying back.

Then comes the repayment schedule. Think of it like a calendar that keeps track of when and how much of your loan you need to repay. Typically, you chip away at your debt with regular payments—maybe every month.

Borrowing: Do it Responsibly

Borrowing isn't the villain here, but borrowing way more than you can handle—that's where things can get messy. It's crucial to borrow sensibly.

Responsible borrowing is all about knowing your limits. Make sure you're borrowing an amount you can repay without burning a hole in your pocket. If you bite off more than you can chew, you could end up with a messed up credit score or even in the red zone known as bankruptcy.

But don't stress! We're just helping you stay in the know. Keeping these things in mind will help you make wiser financial decisions in the future.

The Many Types of Debt

Personal Loans

Picture personal loans as the dolphins of the debt ocean. They're usually friendly, helpful creatures that come to your rescue when you're in a tight spot. Got a car that's given up the ghost? Or a sudden expense that your savings can't cover? A personal loan might be your lifesaver.

These loans are money borrowed from a bank, credit union, or online lender that you can use for many different purposes. You pay them back in monthly installments over a period of time, usually between two to five years. But remember, like a dolphin can pack a punch with its tail, personal loans come with interest rates. And those rates can vary based on your credit score and other factors. So, it's important to shop around and find the best rates before diving in.

Credit Cards

Next up, let's talk about credit cards. Imagine them as magic cards that let you snag that must-have gadget or those killer sneakers, without having to pay up front. Sounds pretty sweet, right?

But don't let the glitz fool you. Credit cards can charge some of the highest interest rates of any type of debt. It's how they make their money. If you don't pay off your balance in full every month, you'll start racking up interest, and that can add up really fast. Credit cards are handy tools, but like any magic, they should be used wisely.

Mortgages

Mortgages are colossal loans that you take out to buy a house, and they're usually paid back over a long period—think 15 to 30 years. If owning a home is in your future plans, then a mortgage will likely be part of that journey.

But remember, mortgages are a long-term commitment. They come with interest rates, and over time, you'll end up paying back much more than you borrowed. Plus, if you don't keep up with your payments, the bank could take your house, a process known as foreclosure. So, while they're a necessary part of home ownership for most people, they're definitely a type of debt you want to handle responsibly.

Student Loans

Finally, we have student loans. They're like that college friend who's super fun at parties but might overstay their welcome at your apartment. Student loans exist to help fund your higher education—college, graduate school, and sometimes even private K-12 education.

The great thing about student loans is that they often have lower interest rates than other types of debt. Plus, you usually don't have to start paying them back until after you graduate.

But here's the catch: they can stick around for a long time. Most student loans have repayment terms between 10 to 30 years. That's a long time to be paying for those frat parties and late-night pizza runs. So, while they can be helpful in getting that degree, remember to borrow responsibly and understand what you're signing up for. Stick around for chapter 11 where we talk about how to finance your education and go about student loans safely and smartly.

Nailing Debt Management

Dealing with debt might seem like you're trying to calm a wild, snarling beast. But remember, even beasts can be tamed. You just need the right strategy. The golden rule? Make your payments on time. It's a bit like homework; turning it in late can cost you marks. In this case, your credit score could take a hit.

Here's a trick that could make it easier for you. Try setting reminders on your phone for when it's time to make payments. Or better yet, set up automatic payments if your bank offers this feature. That way, you won't miss a deadline even if you wanted to!

Say No to Unnecessary Debt

Just like you wouldn't buy an extra-large soda when a regular one quenches your thirst, not all debt is necessary. If your wallet's giving you warning signs, listen. If you're considering taking on debt for something you don't really need, hit the brakes. Saving up for that item or waiting until you can comfortably afford it without debt might be the smarter move.

When Debt Turns Rocky

Dealing with debt can sometimes feel like trying to out-climb a landslide. If it's starting to feel like you're caught in an avalanche, don't panic. There are always options.

Consider getting in touch with a credit counselor. They're like personal trainers for your debt, helping you build a strong game plan to tackle it. They can guide you on creating a budget, offer you free educational materials and workshops, and help you tackle your debt problems.

Another option to consider when you're knee-deep in debt could be debt consolidation. It's a way of combining multiple debts into one single payment. It's like turning a mountain of homework into one manageable assignment.

But remember, you're not alone in this. There are resources and people out there who can help. Don't be afraid to reach out and ask for help. You're stronger than your debt and, with the right plan and support, you can totally beat this!

Debit and Credit Cards: The Dynamic Duo

Okay, pals, time for a little chit-chat about these two essential pieces of plastic in your wallet – debit and credit cards. What are they, and what do they do?

Debit cards are like your trustworthy best friend. You go shopping, it pays right away, using the money straight from your bank account. It's straightforward – you're spending your own money, and there's no debt to worry about.

Credit cards, however, are more like your unpredictable, fun cousin. They let you buy things right now, but you pay for it later. So, basically, you're borrowing money every time you swipe. It's like a thrill ride, but remember, thrill rides can get scary quickly if you go overboard.

Debit vs Credit: The Face-off

Now, let's put these two side by side and see how they measure up.

Debit cards are pretty hassle-free and keep you grounded. You can only spend what you've got in your account, so you're in control. But remember, they don't offer much help if you need to make a large purchase and your account is running low.

Credit cards are more flexible. They can be a life-saver for emergency expenses or when cash is short. Plus, they can boost your credit score if used smartly. But be warned, they can also lead to overspending, and the additional interest can mean you pay back way more.

Using Debit and Credit Cards: The Smart Way

So how can you be a whiz at using these cards? First up, avoid any extra fees like a dodgeball. Know your bank's terms and conditions. Some banks might charge for certain transactions, and you definitely don't want any nasty surprises.

Next, know your limits. This is super important for credit cards. That "buy now, pay later" might sound awesome, but remember, later comes sooner than you think!

And for those of you wielding credit cards, it's crucial to understand interest rates. If you don't pay off your balance each month, you're going to get hit with interest, and those can pile up faster than dirty laundry.

In a nutshell, both debit and credit cards can be your best buddies when it comes to managing your finances, as long as you use them with care.

Case Study: Winning the Debt Game

Who doesn't love a good story, right? This time, it's all about Tom, a young dude who crushed his debt and used credit like a pro. Let's dive into his journey, shall we?

Tom was a college sophomore when he got his first credit card. It was shiny, cool, and boy, it was tempting! He could buy stuff now and pay later, what could possibly go wrong?

At first, Tom used his card responsibly – paying for groceries, textbooks, the usual. He felt pretty grown-up, managing his money like an adult. But soon, he started using it for non-essentials, stuff like video games, takeout every other night... you get the picture.

Before he knew it, Tom had racked up a pretty hefty bill. Worse yet, he couldn't afford to pay it off in full every month. This is where the ugly interest beast showed its face. Every month, his debt seemed to grow faster than a Chia Pet. Panic set in.

But Tom was determined not to let this situation get the best of him. He hatched a plan, aiming to beat his debt and regain control over his finances.

First, Tom put a halt to his spend-fest. He started using his credit card only for essentials, just like in the good old days. He also started using his debit card more to avoid racking up additional debt.

Next, he set up a budget. He allocated money for bills, groceries, and a little for fun stuff, but he made sure he had enough to make larger payments towards his credit card debt each month.

On top of this, Tom picked up a part-time job. The extra cash helped him pay off his debt faster and gave him some breathing room in his budget.

Fast forward a year, and Tom had paid off his debt completely. He had learned his lesson and knew how to use his credit card responsibly. His credit score was back on track, and his financial health was better than ever.

Now, Tom is debt-free and savvy about his spending. He uses his credit card as a tool, not a ticket to buy whatever he wants. He understands the importance of paying off his balance each month to avoid interest charges. And most importantly, he feels empowered and in control of his finances.

Tom's story is a great example of overcoming financial hurdles. He made mistakes (we all do), but he also took responsibility, made a plan, and stuck to it. And if Tom can do it, you can too. We all have the power to take control of our money and make it work for us.

But remember, his story doesn't end here. Once he paid off his debt, he had another task to tackle: rebuilding his credit score.

Why is that important? Well, you're about to find out. In the next chapter, we'll take a deep dive into credit scores: what they are, why they matter, and how you can keep yours in good shape. Get ready to delve into the heart of the financial world, where numbers can make or break opportunities. Your credit score is more than just a three-digit number—it's your financial identity card, your ticket to the world of financial opportunities. Stay tuned, because we're about to reveal the playbook of credit scores!

Chapter 11 - The Credit Score Playbook

All About Credit: Reports, Scores, and Why They Matter

Think about your favorite online game. You know, the one with all the badges, achievements, and high scores? Picture your profile on there, showing all the epic battles you've won, the dragons you've tamed, and the towering castles you've built. Now, imagine something quite similar, but it's all about your real-life money game. This is what we call a credit report.

A credit report is a snapshot of your financial achievements. It narrates your financial journey – from your credit card debt levels, student loans, or that nifty car you're paying off. If there are any missteps, like missed payments, or if anyone's been doing a background check on you (like landlords or banks), that's on there too.

Now, why's this important? Here's the deal: Your credit report is like your trust leaderboard in the financial game. Banks, landlords, and sometimes even bosses peek at it to gauge if you're a champ at handling your cash. If you're dreaming of that shiny new ride or your first cool pad, the lenders will likely review your credit report before handing you the keys. Spotted missed payments might make them twitchy about lending to you, because, hey, they want to be sure they'll get their money back on time!

Even some job roles want to check out your credit report. They reckon how you deal with money could hint at how responsible you might be on the job.

Cracking the Code: Credit Scores Unveiled

A credit score is a number, usually between 300 and 850, acting as your trustworthiness gauge to potential lenders. The higher your score, the more they'll feel confident lending to you.

You're probably thinking, "Who's keeping the score?" It's not a random number bot. Your score is determined by several factors.

First off, your payment history. If you're boss-level at paying bills on time, fantastic! That's gonna hike up your score. Next, your credit utilization – how much of your available credit you're using. Lower usage generally gives your score a boost.

But there's more to it! The length of your credit history matters, too. The longer you've had credit, the better your score. Also, the variety of credit types you have and any fresh credit applications can influence it.

So, why care about the score? A high score can help you level up in real life. It can make getting a loan or a credit card smoother, and you might even score lower interest rates.

Crafting a Stellar Credit Score: Your Game Plan

Kicking off your credit journey can seem like you're on level one of the hardest game ever, staring at a boss battle way above your level. But don't fret! We've got your walkthrough guide ready, with the pro tips you'll need to power up your credit score.

Step one, get some credit. Maybe that's a credit card or a small loan. But remember, it's not an all-access pass to buy everything your heart desires. It's more like a side quest. You make a few manageable purchases, and then, it's time for the important part - paying them off. Yes, you got it, right on time, every single time. Doing this consistently starts building your credit history, which is a huge part of your credit score.

On to the next stage, aim to keep your credit card balance low. A good guideline is to use less than 30% of your credit limit. Let's say your credit card has a limit of $1000, aim to keep your balance under $300. And remember, having a credit card doesn't mean you're required to use it all the time.

Here's another tip, don't shut down old credit accounts, even if they're collecting dust. They add to the length of your credit history, which can help level up your score.

The last bit of advice, keep a close watch on your credit report. You can typically get a free one from each credit bureau every year. It's like checking your game stats, seeing where you can improve. If you notice something off, there are ways to correct mistakes and protect your score. And guess what, you've got legal power-ups to help! You have rights concerning your credit report, so don't hesitate to use them.

And there you have it, your guide to building a great credit score. It might feel like you're scaling a mountain, but with patience, good practices, and regular checks, you'll reach that peak in no time. Remember, every player starts at level one.

When Things Go South: Bouncing Back from Bad Credit

Okay, let's tackle a tougher topic. Having a bad credit score can feel like the end of the world. But remember, you can always hit reset and start working to improve your situation.

So, what's bad credit? Imagine if the game of credit gave you a score from 300 to 850, and you're stuck with a score that's closer to 300. Not the best feeling, right? That's what having bad credit is like. It usually happens when you've had a tough time keeping up with payments or if you've borrowed more than you can handle.

The effects of bad credit can be a bit of a downer. It can make it harder to get loans or credit cards, and if you do get them, you might have to pay higher interest rates. It can even impact other areas of life, like getting a job or renting an apartment. So, yeah, it's something you want to avoid if you can. But if you're already there, it's not game over!

Now, onto the good part - fixing bad credit. Here are a few steps you can take:

1. Catch up on payments as soon as you can:

2. Make sure to make all your payments on time from now on. It's the easiest way to start gaining points.

3. Try to keep the balance on your credit cards low. It shows you're managing your current level before moving on to the next one.

4. Create a budget to help you figure out how much you can spend and save.

5. Seek professional help from credit counselors who can offer valuable advice on building back your credit score.

Remember, repairing bad credit takes time and patience, but you'll get there. After all, everyone loves a good comeback story, right? Just keep at it, and over time, you'll see your score start to climb.

And boom! We've just dived head-first into the deep end of the credit pool and made it back up to the surface. We've broken down the nitty-gritty of credit scores, figured out what happens when credit goes south, and learned how to bounce back like a boss.

Remember, all this info isn't just cool to know—it's a financial life vest. This knowledge could keep you from plunging into the deep, dark ocean of debt and bad credit.

So, as we wrap up this chapter, you're not just an onlooker anymore—you're the captain of your own financial ship, ready to sail the high seas of credit.

But here's the thing: knowing the theory and putting it into action are two different ball games. That's why we've got something fun lined up in the next chapter—a mini-quiz we're calling "Ready, Set, Recall!". It's the perfect pit-stop for you to revise and remember all the killer advice you've picked up in Part 4.

So bring your best game face, and let's get recalling!

Ready, Set, Recall

Let's get cracking on this quiz for Part 4 - Borrowing and Credit. This is your chance to see how well you've been soaking up all the info on borrowing and credit scores. Don't stress out if you don't get everything right at first. It's all part of the learning process. And remember, the answer key is tucked away in the resources section at the back.

Quiz for Part 4 - Borrowing and Credit

1. What's the difference between a debit card and a credit card?
    a) There's no difference
    b) A debit card lets you borrow money, a credit card does not
    c) A credit card lets you borrow money, a debit card does not
    d) Debit cards are only for online shopping

2. Which one of these is NOT a type of debt?
    a) Mortgage
    b) Auto Loan
    c) Birthday Present
    d) Student Loan

3. What does it mean to manage your debt?
    a) Paying all your debts at once
    b) Never getting into debt
    c) Making sure you pay your debts on time and effectively reducing what

you owe over time

    d) Borrowing more money to pay off your debt

4. What's a credit score?

    a) A rating that determines your trustworthiness as a borrower

    b) A score you get on your math test

    c) The amount of credit cards you have

    d) A number that represents your total debt

5. What can impact your credit score?

    a) Paying your bills on time

    b) The amount of debt you have

    c) How long you've had credit for

    d) All of the above

6. How can you improve your credit score?

    a) Taking on more debt

    b) Paying your bills late

    c) Paying your bills on time, keeping your balance low, and being cautious about opening new credit cards

    d) Closing all your credit cards

7. Can your credit score affect your ability to get a loan or credit card?

    a) No, credit scores have no impact on loans or credit cards

    b) Yes, your credit score can impact your ability to get a loan or credit card and the interest rate you're offered

    c) No, only your job status affects your ability to get a loan or credit card

    d) Yes, but only if you're applying for a car loan

8. What should you do if you have a bad credit score?

    a) Ignore it, it'll get better on its own

    b) Take steps to improve it, like paying bills on time, reducing debt, and avoiding new debt

c) Apply for as many credit cards as possible to increase your score

d) Declare bankruptcy

9. Why is it important to read the terms and conditions before taking on new debt?

a) It's not important, just sign and figure it out later

b) The terms and conditions outline important details like interest rates, penalties, and fees

c) To check if there are any hidden rewards

d) Only to check the due date

10. How can you check your credit score?

a) Ask a friend

b) Request a report from a credit bureau or use a reputable online service

c) Check the bottom of your bank statement

d) You can't, it's confidential information

Enjoying and Finding Value in Our Book?

We're thrilled that you've journeyed through the first part of The Essential Money Skills Handbook for Teens. By now, we hope you've started unraveling the mysteries of personal finance and begun to understand the importance of money management. If the book has been insightful and beneficial in guiding you on your financial journey, we'd greatly appreciate your support.

Could you take a moment to leave a review? It only takes a minute, but your feedback could help countless other teenagers gain confidence in managing their money and planning their financial futures. Your words matter, not just to us, but to future readers who could benefit from the same knowledge you've gained.

Thank you for investing your time with us and in your financial future. We look forward to hearing your thoughts and comments!

Customer reviews

★★★★☆ 4.7 out of 5

221 global ratings

5 star		76%
4 star		20%
3 star		3%
2 star		1%
1 star		1%

∨ How customer reviews and ratings work

Review this product

Share your thoughts with other customers

Write a customer review

Scan this QR code to leave a 1-minute review!

Your feedback is incredibly valuable, not only for us but also for other parents and educators seeking guidance on financial literacy for teens. By sharing your thoughts, you'll contribute to the growth and improvement of RaiseYouthRight. Our hope is that with the information we share, we can make the next generation healthier, wealthier, and happier than ours!

We appreciate your support and look forward to diving into Part 2, where we'll explore practical ways to apply these valuable career planning tools.

V

Part 5 - Charting Your Course: Finances for Life's Big Moments

Chapter 12 - Financing Your Education: Student Loans and Scholarships

H ey there, future college superstar! You know that big, exciting, maybe a little-bit-scary world called college that's right around the corner? We're about to dive into one of the biggest parts of it - the moolah, the dough, the cash...in other words, the finances. But hold up, don't freak out just yet! This chapter's going to be your best buddy in figuring out how to fund your dreams without selling a kidney.

Alright, let's get real for a sec. College can be pricy (no surprise there), but luckily there's this nifty thing called student loans. And scholarships. And grants. Lots of options, really. They can be a lifesaver when you're eyeing that intimidating tuition bill. But with great power comes great responsibility, right? You'll have to pay back those loans eventually, so it's important to understand how they work.

From the basic lowdown on federal versus private loans to the details on deferment and loan forgiveness (yep, that's a thing), we're going to take a walk through all of it. Plus, we'll talk about how to score that free money - scholarships and grants. Sound like a plan?

So buckle up, get comfy, and let's get this show on the road. You're about to become a whizz at this whole college financing thing, promise.

Navigating the World of Student Loans

Alright! Let's dig into this whole student loans thing. Picture this: you're dreaming about college, but the costs seem out of this world, right? Enter student loans. Swooping in to cover those sky-high costs and letting you pay them back bit by bit, plus some extra (that's what we call interest).

The Tale of Two Loans: Federal vs. Private

Let's break it down into the two main characters in our student loans story: federal and private loans. Federal loans come from the government. They've got fixed interest rates (that means they won't change on you) and flexible repayment plans. Private loans, on the other hand, are from private lenders like banks or credit unions. They're a bit like a choose-your-own-adventure book, with interest rates and terms that can change big time.

Decoding Loan Lingo: Subsidized and Unsubsidized Loans

Now, let's decode some loan jargon: subsidized and unsubsidized. Both come from the government, but there's a key difference. With subsidized loans, the government has your back, covering your interest while you're in school and during certain other periods. Unsubsidized loans? Not so much. The interest starts racking up from the get-go.

Student Loans: The Good, the Bad, and the Necessary

So, student loans can be your ticket to college. They can cover those costs when you're a little short on cash. But remember, borrowing money is a pretty big decision. You'll need to pay it back eventually, and the longer it takes, the more you'll owe because of interest. But if it helps you get that degree and score your dream job, it could totally be worth it.

The Student Loan Quest: How to Apply

Okay, so you're ready to embark on your student loan quest? Awesome! For federal loans, your journey starts with the FAFSA, which tells you how much you can borrow. If you're eyeing private loans, you'll need to explore a bit. Different lenders have different rules, so find one that works for you. Once you've chosen, fill out their application and keep your fingers crossed. Just remember, take it slow, and make sure you understand what you're signing up for. It's not a race.

Cracking the Code of Your Student Loan Repayment Plan

Picture this. You've graduated, tossed your cap in the air, and then...bam! Your student loans say "hi" and remind you it's time to start repaying. But what does that mean? Let's unbox this. Your repayment plan is like your game plan for paying off your loans. It sets out how much you'll pay each month, and for how long. Sounds simple, right? Well, let's dive a little deeper.

The Road Map to Repayment: Choosing Your Route

There are a few paths you can choose for your repayment journey. The 'standard' route means you'll pay the same amount every month. Then there's the 'graduated' route, where your payments start off small and grow over time. On the 'extended' route, you'll be paying for a longer time, but with smaller payments. Then there are 'income-driven' plans, where your payment changes with your income. It's like choosing your own adventure, but with money!

Loan Forgiveness Programs: The Golden Ticket

Let's talk about a dream scenario. Imagine someone telling you, "Hey, you know that money you owe us? Nevermind. You don't have to pay it back." Sounds fantastic, right? That's pretty much what loan forgiveness programs are. They can erase some, or even all, of your student loans if you meet certain requirements. Usually, this means working in public service or teaching in certain areas for a set period. To apply, you need to fill out some paperwork, so if you think you might qualify, get on it!

Taking a Breather: Deferment and Forbearance

Now, let's say life throws a curveball your way, and you need to hit the pause button on your loan payments. That's where deferment and forbearance come in. They let you take a break from making payments for a bit. The difference? With deferment, you might not have to pay the interest that builds up during your break. With forbearance, you're on the hook for all of it. But remember, these should be your last resort. They can help in a pinch, but the longer you take to repay, the more you'll pay in the long run.

The Scary Side of Student Loans: Delinquency and Default

Let's talk about the elephant in the room: what happens if you can't pay your student loans? If you're late on a payment, you become 'delinquent.' If you keep missing payments, you could go into 'default,' which is as scary as it sounds. Your wages could be garnished, your credit score could take a hit, and it could take years to get out of it. So, don't ignore your loans. If you're having trouble making payments, reach out to your loan servicer. They can help you figure out your options.

Scholarships vs. Grants: Two Different Paths to "Free Money"

When it comes to college funding, "free money" sounds too good to be true, right? But it's not a myth. Scholarships and grants are both ways to bankroll your education without taking on debt. The key difference? Scholarships are usually merit-based, meaning they're awarded based on things like grades, athletic ability, or talent in the arts. On the flip side, grants are typically need-based, given to students who can demonstrate financial need.

The Treasure Hunt: Searching for Scholarships

Think of hunting for scholarships like an epic treasure hunt, where X marks the spot for free money. So, where do you start? There's a whole universe of scholarships out there, from local community organizations to big national companies. Some universities even offer their own scholarships. To apply, you'll typically need to fill out an application, and often, write an essay or provide references. So, get out there and start hunting!

Crafting a Winning Application: Your Personal Highlight Reel

Applying for a scholarship isn't just about ticking boxes. You want to stand out from the crowd. Think of your application as your personal highlight reel. Showcase your strengths, passion, and what makes you unique. And don't forget to proofread! Nothing says "I'm not serious" like typos and grammatical errors.

Navigating the World of Grants: Federal, State, and College-Specific

Grants are a bit like financial guardian angels, swooping in to help those who need it. Federal grants come from Uncle Sam, and they're generally the largest. State grants vary by where you live or plan to go to school. College-specific grants come directly from the school you attend. To apply for most grants, you'll need to fill out the Free Application for Federal Student Aid (FAFSA), so make sure to have that on your to-do list.

Securing Grants: Your Strategy for Success

When it comes to successfully landing grants, strategy is everything. First off, apply as early as you can. The early bird gets the worm, or in this case, the grant money. Make sure you have all the necessary documents ready to go and fill out the application carefully. Finally, don't forget to showcase your need and your dedication to your studies. After all, grants are there to help students who need it and are willing to put in the work. Happy hunting!

Deciding How Much to Borrow: The Future's Looking Bright!

Here's the thing - borrowing money for college is a bit like trying to see the future. You've got to make a guess about your earning potential after graduation. What kind of job will you land? How much will it pay? Will you be rolling in money or living paycheck to paycheck? It's not an exact science, but looking at the average salaries in your desired field can give you a ballpark figure. Aim to borrow only as much as you think you'll comfortably be able to pay back with your future earnings. It's like having a crystal ball for your finances.

The Long-Game: Student Loans, Your Future, and Your Feelings

Okay, let's not beat around the bush. Student loans can feel like a massive boulder on your future. We're talking about more than just numbers on a bank statement. We're talking about late-night worries, stress sweats, and that knot in your stomach when the loan repayment notification pops up. But here's the truth: these feelings? They're normal. Yep, you heard it right. Normal.

These loans can put a dent in your credit score and can potentially put a pause on big life moves, like getting that cool condo downtown or upgrading to a slick new car. They might even sneak into your daydreams and become your most disliked monthly bill. Yup, it's not just you. We all get the jitters when it comes to debt.

But hey, take a deep breath. It's not all doom and gloom! With the right repayment plan, student loans can totally be handled. And you know what's the best part? That feeling when you make that last payment. Ah, the relief! The pride! The freedom! It's like standing on a mountain peak after a tough climb.

And you want to know a secret? It's not just about the numbers. It's about building resilience, about facing challenges head-on. And remember, every successful repayment is a step closer to that mountaintop. So, prepare for the journey, buckle up, and remember: you're not alone in this. The road might be long and winding, but believe us, the view from the top? Totally worth it.

The Road Less Traveled: Alternatives to Student Loans

Student loans may seem like the go-to option for college financing, but they're not the only game in town. Work-study programs offer a chance to earn money for college while gaining valuable experience. Part-time jobs during school or summer vacations can also help cushion your college fund. Heck, some people even crowdfund their college tuition. It's 2023, after all! Explore your options. There's more than one way to finance your education.

Real Talk: Balancing Scholarships, Grants, and Loans

Okay, now let's dive into some real-life scenarios. Meet Alex. She got a few scholarships, and a grant, and decided to borrow the rest in student loans. She balanced her financing options and ended up with a manageable amount of debt. Then there's Jordan. He didn't qualify for many scholarships or grants but took on a part-time job to offset the loans he had to take. Both found their own way to finance their education and made it work for their personal situations.

The Bottom Line: Financing Your Education Wisely

So here's the deal - financing your education is like about balancing scholarships, grants, loans, and maybe a part-time job. It's about thinking about your future earnings and making sure you're not digging a financial hole you can't climb out of. It's not easy, but hey, neither is college. And you're about to conquer that. You've got this. Just remember, be smart, do your research, and make the choices that are right for you. It's your future after all. And it's looking pretty bright.

Chapter 13 - Playing the Long Game: Start Your Retirement Journey Now

Why It's Essential to Start Retirement Planning Early

You know how in superhero movies, the protagonist starts training way before the big showdown? That's exactly what retirement planning is like. You're the superhero, and retirement is that climactic fight scene. Only, instead of cosmic energy or super strength, you're gearing up with money. Sounds a bit dull, right? It's anything but.

Retirement might feel like a speck on the horizon when you're in your teens or early twenties, but it's coming, just like that final battle. And when it arrives, you want to be ready to embrace it, not fret about how you're going to manage without a steady income. The more time you give yourself, the easier it's going to be to build up a retirement fund that'll let you kick back and enjoy your golden years.

By starting early, you give your savings more time to grow. Think of it like planting a tree. If you plant a sapling today, it'll grow into a sturdy tree over the years, providing shade and fruits. Your retirement fund is that sapling. Given time and consistent care (read: regular contributions), it'll grow into a financial support system for your future self. Cool, huh?

Understanding the Concept of the Time Value of Money

So, we've established that time is your friend when planning for retirement. But why is that? Here's where we introduce a little something called the 'time value of money.'

Imagine this: You've got a comic book worth $10. You could sell it now, pocket the ten bucks, and maybe spend it on that fast food meal you've been craving. But what if you hold onto it? In a few years, that comic book could become a collector's item worth $100. If you'd sold it earlier, you would've missed out on the extra $90. This, my friends, is a simple illustration of the time value of money.

In finance terms, the time value of money suggests that a dollar today is worth more than the same dollar in the future. That's because of inflation (prices generally go up over time) and the potential earning capacity of that dollar if you invest it.

When it comes to retirement planning, understanding the time value of money helps you grasp why starting early is a super move. By investing your money, you give it the chance to grow over time. And with more time, you have more opportunities to multiply your money and defeat the villainous inflation.

Mastering the Long Game: Your Long-Term Financial Strategy

Think about your life as an epic movie. Each scene, each decision, creates a path toward your grand finale. Your long-term financial strategy? Well, that's the script you're writing to guide you there. And the sooner you start, the better the plot turns out!

When we talk about long-term financial planning, we're referring to the big picture of your financial life. Imagine this as a giant treasure map, marking down dreams and goals like buying your first car, paying for college, or even launching your own business. Yes, retirement too—because who doesn't want their golden years to shine bright?

Now, the cool part about this treasure map is that it gives you control. Think of yourself as the mapmaker and the explorer, plotting your path and adjusting as needed. It directs your money moves, helping you dodge the unexpected pitfalls (because life loves surprises, right?), and set you on the course towards your dream destination.

The sooner you sketch this map, the more time you'll have to amass your treasure—through the awesome power of savings and compound interest. But more on that soon!

The Role of Saving and Investing in Long-Term Financial Planning

As you set sail on your financial journey, savings act like your trusted compass—essential for any explorer. The money you squirrel away helps you reach your financial goals. Without it, your journey might stall before you've even left the dock.

But here's the secret to turbocharging your journey: saving alone isn't enough. Investing is your ship's sails, catching the wind and propelling you forward, often at a much quicker pace than savings alone. Stick around for part 6 for the low-down on investing and how powerful it can be.

Investing may feel a bit like braving uncharted waters, but with a long-term view and a little learning (or maybe some help from a financial guide), it can be an amazing way to grow your treasure.

Together, saving and investing are your trusty crew, working hand in hand to keep you on course toward your financial goals. And remember, it's cool if you don't know it all yet. This adventure is all about learning as you go.

Understanding Retirement Accounts

We've got your attention on this retirement thing, right? Awesome! Now, let's zoom in on a special tool designed to help you prepare for that future beach house or cabin in the woods (or whatever your dream retirement looks like): retirement accounts.

An Overview of Various Retirement Accounts (401k, IRA, Roth IRA, etc.)

Think of a retirement account as a special savings jar that keeps growing over time. And the best bit? And sometimes, you won't even have to share any of your savings with the taxman! Sounds fun, doesn't it? Let's understand the different types of these special jars.

Firstly, there's something called a 401(k). This is usually given by your work and it allows you to save a piece of your income before taxes are deducted. The most thrilling part? Sometimes your boss will add some extra cash matching what you put in. That's like receiving bonus money for when you grow old!

Next, there's something known as an Individual Retirement Account, or IRA for short. There are two sorts - Traditional and Roth. With a Traditional IRA, you put in money that you possibly won't have to pay taxes on, and any interest it earns might also grow without taxes until you need it when you're older.

Roth IRAs work a bit differently. You put in money that you've already paid taxes on, but when you become old and require the money, you can take it out without paying any more taxes! This could be excellent if you believe you're paying less in taxes now than you might in your older years.

Which special jar should you pick, you wonder? That's a brilliant question. Each one has its own unique traits and things to think about.

A 401(k) is super because your boss might give you extra cash. However, you might only have a few choices on how to grow your savings.

Traditional IRAs allow you to pick how you wish to grow your savings, and you might not have to pay taxes on the money you put in. But when you withdraw the money when you're older, you most likely will have to pay taxes on it.

Roth IRAs allow you to withdraw money tax-free when you're older, which is super neat. But, you pay taxes on your savings before you put it in, and only people who earn a certain level of income or more can have a Roth IRA.

Choosing the right retirement account depends on you. Consider how much taxes you're paying now, how much you guess you'll pay when you're older, and how much you want to decide on how to grow your savings. And don't forget, you can have more than one kind of jar. Starting to save early and regularly in these special jars can help you amass a gigantic treasure by the time you're older!

Social Security 101

Imagine you've entered the time machine and zoomed into the future. You've hung up your work hat, kicked back, and now it's all about enjoying the fruits of your years of hard work. You're retired! Now, how do you keep the money flowing in? One of the key players here is something called Social Security, and we're going to take a tour of what it's all about.

What is Social Security and Who is Eligible?

Okay, so Social Security is like this big money pool set up by the government, and it's got your back when you retire, or if you become disabled. Think of it like this – a chunk of your paycheck, while you're working, takes a slide into this pool. When it's time to retire, you start getting payments from it.

Who can get these payments, you ask? Mostly people who have worked and contributed to Social Security for enough years. You need 40 'credits' to be in the club, and you can bag up to 4 credits per year. So, 10 years of work? Boom, you're in!

How Does Social Security Work and How are Benefits Calculated?

So, if everyone's paying in, does everyone get the same amount back? Nope, it's not a flat-rate club. The money you get depends on your lifetime earnings, when you decide to retire, and how long you've paid into the system. Your 35 highest-earning years are considered when calculating your benefits. So, the more moolah you make and the longer you work, the fatter your Social Security checks can be.

When and How to Apply for Social Security Benefits

Now, the golden question: when do you get to see the money? You can start getting benefits from age 62, but wait, there's a bit of a twist. If you start taking money before your 'full retirement age' (which is between 66 and 67 for most people), your monthly checks will be a bit smaller. If you can hold off a little longer, your benefit gets a boost for every year you wait, up to age 70.

When it's go time, applying for benefits is as simple as doing it online, on the phone, or at a local Social Security office. Remember to apply a few months before you want to start receiving benefits.

The Role of Social Security in Your Overall Retirement Planning

So how does Social Security fit into your big picture of retirement? It's an important piece, but remember, it's just one piece of your retirement pie. It's meant to replace only a part of your pre-retirement income. For a truly rocking retirement, you'll also want to have some savings, investments, and perhaps a retirement account or two.

And that, my friend, is your crash course in Social Security. By getting the scoop now, you're already lapping many in the race toward a sweet retirement.

Pensions and Employer-Sponsored Retirement Plans

Pop quiz: Imagine your future self - you know, the one that's living it up in retirement. Where's the money coming from? Social Security? Check. Savings and investments? Check. But what about pensions and employer-sponsored retirement plans? If you just tilted your head and said, "huh?" then we got a new topic to tackle. So, let's dive in!

Understanding What a Pension is and How It Works

First, let's decode this mysterious thing called a pension. A pension is kinda like a promise. It's your employer saying, "Hey, thanks for your years of service. Here's a steady stream of income when you retire." This flow of cash comes from a fund your employer contributes to while you're working.

Now, the exact details can vary. Sometimes, it's a defined benefit plan, which means you'll get a specific amount each month after you retire. The amount is usually based on your salary, and how long you've been with the company. Other times, it's a defined contribution plan, where you (and sometimes your employer) throw money into a retirement account, like a 401(k) (don't worry, we'll talk about that too).

The Benefits of Employer-Sponsored Retirement Plans and How to Make the Most of Them

Speaking of 401ks, let's chat about employer-sponsored retirement plans. These plans, including 401ks, 403bs, and others, are like superpowers for your retirement savings. They let you put away money from your paycheck, pre-tax, which means you could pay less income tax now. Plus, your money grows tax-free until you withdraw it at retirement. And, here's the real kicker, many employers will match a portion of your contributions.

So, how do you make the most of these plans? First, if your employer offers a match, aim to contribute at least enough to snag the full match. It's the quickest way to turbo-boost your savings. Second, don't be tempted to withdraw early, as that can lead to penalties and taxes.

Now, don't fret if you change jobs. You usually have a few options, including leaving the money where it is, rolling it over into a new employer's plan, or rolling it over into an Individual Retirement Account (IRA). Remember, this is your future we're talking about. So, take some time to understand your options, ask for advice if needed, and make the choice that's best for you.

And there you have it! Pensions and employer-sponsored retirement plans decoded. Just another way you're setting yourself up for future success.

Retirement Lifestyle Planning

Now, let's get real. Your dream lifestyle is going to cost money. That peaceful beach might be in an area with high living costs. Traveling the world isn't cheap. And even a cozy home has expenses - utilities, maintenance, property taxes just to name a few. Retirement isn't just a long vacation; it's a whole stage of life, with its own set of costs. And don't forget about healthcare; it tends to get pricier as we age.

So, how do you plan for this? Start by brainstorming what you want your retirement lifestyle to look like. Then, do a bit of research to estimate how much it'll cost. Remember, it's okay to make educated guesses. You're not writing a contract in stone; you're creating a roadmap to guide you.

How to Estimate Your Retirement Income Needs

Alright, so you've got an idea of your dream retirement lifestyle. Now, let's talk about how much income you'll need to fund it. This is where it gets a bit tricky because there are so many factors at play. Will you have a paid-off home, or will you be renting? What about medical expenses? And don't forget inflation - the rising cost of living over time.

A common rule of thumb is to aim for about 70-80% of your pre-retirement income. So, if you're earning $50,000 a year before you retire, you might aim for around $35,000 to $40,000 a year in retirement. Why less? Well, hopefully, by retirement, you'll have fewer expenses - no more commuting costs, work clothes, and with some good planning, no more mortgage!

Remember, this is a very rough estimate. It's a starting point. You might need more if you plan to travel a lot, or less if you plan to live a simple life. The key is to start thinking about it now, and adjust your plans as you go along.

So, there you go, retirement lifestyle planning in a nutshell. Sure, it might feel a bit like gazing into a crystal ball, but it's really about making the best plans you can with the information you have. And who knows, with some good planning and a bit of luck, your retirement might just turn out better than you imagined!

Non-Traditional Retirement Planning: Real Estate, Entrepreneurship, and More

Okay, let's spice things up a bit. You now know about the traditional ways of planning for retirement, like those employer-sponsored 401ks and IRAs. But did you know there are also non-traditional ways to feather your retirement nest? Yep, things like real estate, entrepreneurship, and more can also become parts of your retirement master plan. Let's dive into these exciting options!

Discussing Non-Traditional Retirement Plans Such as Income From Real Estate or a Business

So, what's the deal with these non-traditional retirement plans? Well, they're about more than just saving money. They're about growing it in ways that also let you flex your creative muscles or follow your passions. Cool, right?

Imagine owning a house or apartment, not just to live in, but to rent out for extra cash. That's what income from real estate is all about. Or, how about turning that hobby you love, whether it's baking cupcakes or designing video games, into a thriving business? These are active, engaging ways to plan for retirement, and they can make the journey a lot more fun and satisfying.

How These Sources Can Complement Traditional Retirement Plans

You might be wondering, "Why bother with non-traditional plans when I've got my traditional retirement plan all sorted out?" Good question! But think of non-traditional plans like the secret bonus levels in a video game. They can give you an added boost, provide a safety net, or even offer a fresh new challenge.

Let's say you've got a rental property. The rent you collect from your tenants can be a nice supplement to your traditional retirement savings, giving you extra padding for those golden years. Or, your own business can not only add to your retirement funds but also give you a sense of purpose and joy, so you're not just retiring from work, but to something you love.

The bottom line? Non-traditional retirement planning isn't for everyone, but it's worth considering. It can add variety to your retirement game plan, and let's face it, variety is the spice of life!

So, ready to think outside the box and mix up your retirement planning a little?

Leveraging Technology for Retirement Planning and Exploring Sustainable Investment Options

Whoa, hold up. We're talking about technology and retirement planning in the same sentence? You bet! These two seemingly distant things are actually closer than you think. Plus, let's toss in some info about a type of investing that's making quite a buzz these days - sustainable investing. Cool, right?

Leveraging Technology for Retirement Planning

Think of your favorite game. Now, wouldn't it be awesome if planning your retirement was as engaging and user-friendly as that? Well, it can be! There are these things called "robo-advisors". No, they're not robots in suits (sadly), but they are automated platforms that give financial advice or investment management online with little to no human intervention. They're like your personal financial planners, minus the office appointments and suits!

And don't forget about Budgeting apps, investment platforms, and savings trackers - these are all your friends when it comes to managing your money and planning for retirement.

What's more, technology is not just about tools and platforms, it's also a massive library of knowledge. Ever heard of online courses or financial podcasts? They're a super cool way to become a pro at personal finance and retirement planning. So, you're not only managing your money, but you're also learning heaps along the way. Be sure to check out our favorite retirement planning tech in the resources chapter at the end of the book.

Exploring Sustainable and Socially Responsible Investment Options

Okay, let's switch gears a bit and talk about something that's really hitting the headlines these days - sustainable and socially responsible investing (SRI). These are investments in companies or funds that are committed to social, environmental, and ethical causes.

Now, you might be thinking, "What's that got to do with retirement?" Well, SRI can be a part of your retirement portfolio. Diversifying your investments is like trying different dishes at a buffet - it's a wise thing to do. You get a taste of everything without risking a full-blown dislike for a single dish. And in the case of SRI, it feels good too because you're supporting causes you believe in.

But how do you find and evaluate SRI options for your retirement accounts? That's a great question. Research is your best friend here. Look for funds or companies that match your values and see if they fit your financial plan.

In a world where your smartphone is almost an extension of you, technology plays a big role in how you plan for your future. But remember, it's not just about the tech or the cool apps. It's about taking control of your financial future. And if you can support some sustainable causes while doing it, then that's a win-win, right?

Dealing with Retirement Risks

So, we've been talking a lot about the sunshine and rainbows of retirement planning, but let's not ignore the storm clouds. There are risks involved in retirement planning, kinda like those boss battles in video games. But don't worry, just like with gaming, if you know what to expect, you can develop some smart strategies to manage these risks.

Overview of the Potential Risks in Retirement (Longevity Risk, Market Risk, Inflation Risk, Etc.)

Alright, let's break down these big bad boss battles. The first is the longevity risk. This is a fancy way of saying that you might outlive your savings. Yeah, I know, it sounds kind of morbid, but people are living longer these days, which is a good thing! We just have to make sure our money can keep up with us.

Next up is market risk. That's all about the ups and downs of the stock market and how they could affect your retirement funds. Kind of like how a storm could rock your ship on the ocean, unexpected market changes can shake up your savings.

Lastly, we've got the inflation risk. You know how the price of stuff tends to go up over time? That's inflation, and it's like a sneaky thief stealing the value of your money. When you're planning for retirement, you need to think about how inflation might impact the buying power of your savings.

Strategies to Manage These Risks

Alright, now that we know what we're up against, let's talk strategy. For the longevity risk, one approach is to save more and invest wisely to build a larger nest egg. Some people also choose to work part-time in retirement or delay their retirement date.

To combat market risk, a well-diversified portfolio can be your best friend. By spreading your money across different types of investments, you're not putting all your eggs in one basket, which can help you weather market storms.

As for inflation, investing some of your money in assets that tend to increase in value over time, like stocks or real estate, can be a smart move. These types of investments can grow faster than inflation, helping to preserve the buying power of your savings.

Phew! I know, it's a lot to take in, but don't stress. Remember, understanding the risks is half the battle, and now that you're armed with knowledge and strategies, you're already ahead of the game.

Putting It All Together: Creating Your Personal Retirement Plan

Alright, so we've covered a lot, haven't we? Like a whirlwind tour through the Land of Retirement Planning. Now, it's time to take all that knowledge and turn it into a personal retirement plan, your very own treasure map to Future You's dreams.

Step-by-Step Guide to Creating a Personal Retirement Plan Based on the Information Discussed in the Chapter

So where do we start? Well, grab a seat, maybe some snacks (popcorn, anyone?), and let's break this down:

1. **Know Your Goals:** Just like in any epic quest, you need to know your destination. Do you want to travel the world? Start a business? Become a full-time gardener? Make a list of what you want your retirement to look like.

2. **Estimate Your Needs:** Now, think about how much that lifestyle might cost.

Be realistic here and consider everything from basic living expenses to leisure activities.

3. **Assess Your Resources:** Next, consider all potential income sources you might have in retirement. This includes Social Security, pensions, retirement accounts, real estate, etc.

4. **Make a Savings and Investment Plan:** Based on your goals and resources, work out how much you need to save and invest each month to meet your retirement goals.

5. **Consider Your Risk Tolerance**: Remember those retirement risks we talked about? Make sure your plan aligns with how much risk you're comfortable taking.

6. **Choose the Right Retirement Accounts:** Consider your options (like IRAs, 401k, etc.) and choose the ones that best fit your needs.

This isn't a one-and-done sort of thing. You'll be tweaking and changing this plan as your life changes. Which brings us to...

Emphasizing the Importance of Regular Review and Adjustment of the Plan

Your life isn't going to stay the same, and neither should your retirement plan. Maybe you'll get a new job, start a family, win the lottery - who knows! That's why it's crucial to check in on your retirement plan regularly and make adjustments as needed.

Consider it like your favorite game's update patch - it helps improve your plan and keeps it in line with your changing life goals.

And that, my friend, is your blueprint to creating a personalized retirement plan.

Remember, all those dreams you have for your future, those shiny visions of what your life could be? They don't just magically happen. They need a solid plan, determination, and yes, even a little bit of elbow grease. But you've got all that, right? I mean, you're here, aren't you? So, let's make those dreams a reality.

You might be thinking, "But I'm young, I've got loads of time!" And you're right, you do. But here's the thing about time - it sneaks up on you. Before you know it, you'll be asking yourself where all those years went. So why not get a head start? Start now, start today. Your future self will give you a big thumbs up, trust me.

Chapter 14 - Tackling the Giants: How to Plan for Major Expenses

The Big Deal: Cars and Houses

E ver been to a rock concert where the main band totally steals the show? They're the big act, the reason everyone's there. Now, imagine the world of personal finance as a rock concert. The flashy cars and the cozy houses? They're the main acts! They're what we refer to as 'big ticket items'.

Why cars and houses, you ask? Well, it's because these are some of the priciest purchases you're likely to make in your life. We're not just talking about a new gaming console or the latest smartphone. No, these items can cost a small (or sometimes not so small) fortune. And the thing is, most of the time, they're not just wants, they're needs.

Game Plan for Big Buys

So, cars and houses are big deals. Cool. Now, how does one afford these big-ticket items?

First off, plan! It's like heading out on a journey. You wouldn't just hop in a car and drive without a destination in mind, right? So, buying a car or a house is your journey, and you need a clear map of your finances.

Start by setting a budget. Work out how much you can realistically stash away each month towards your mega purchase. And remember, no contribution is too small. It might seem like a drop in the ocean now, but give it time, and it'll start looking more like a sea.

Next up, consider setting up a savings account specifically for this purpose. Watching the total inch up every month can be super motivating, and it also keeps your big purchase fund away from your daily spending money.

And here's something super important – be realistic about what you can afford. Just because you CAN get the flashiest car or the biggest house doesn't mean you SHOULD. I mean, what's the point of having a fancy car or a massive house if you're left eating instant noodles for every meal because all your money is tied up?

Remember, when it comes to these huge purchases, planning and saving are your BFFs.

Shiny New Wheels vs. Trusted Old Steeds

Let's chat about cars, shall we? And no, I don't mean debating if a Lamborghini is cooler than a Bugatti. I'm talking about the age-old question: new or used? When it comes to buying a car, this is the big decision you've got to make.

New Cars: The Good and The Bad

First up, new cars. Oh, the appeal of that new car smell, untouched interiors, and the latest tech features! Plus, with a new car, you get a warranty, which is like a safety net for your car. Something goes wrong in the first couple of years? No problem, the warranty's got your back.

But, (yep, there's always a 'but'), new cars come with a higher price tag. Your wallet will definitely feel the difference. Also, the value of a new car drops faster than a hot potato out of the oven. That's something called depreciation, and it happens super quick with new cars.

Used Cars: The Ups and Downs

On the flip side, we have used cars. These can be lighter on your pocket, which is a huge plus. Plus, they don't depreciate as quickly as new cars do. So, if you sell it a few years down the line, you might get a decent amount back.

But hold up, it's not all sunshine and rainbows with used cars. They may come with a few more miles on the clock, and the chances of mechanical issues pop up can be higher. And unless you're buying a certified pre-owned vehicle, chances are, you're not getting a warranty.

Getting the Money: Loans and Leases

Alright, you've picked your dream car, now how do you pay for it? Most people don't have heaps of cash lying around to buy a car outright, so they turn to financing. Car loans are one way to go. You borrow the money, buy the car, and then pay back the loan over time, with interest, of course.

Another option is leasing. It's kinda like renting. You make monthly payments for a set period, and at the end of the lease, you can either buy the car or give it back. It can be a good option if you like driving newer cars and don't mind not actually owning the vehicle.

So, whether you're all about that new car smell or more into a tried-and-tested ride, remember, both have their pros and cons. And when it comes to paying for it, there's always a way. Just pick what suits you best, and you'll be on the road in no time!

Your First Home: The Rent vs Buy Debate

Are you ready for a change of scenery? Dreaming of your own place? Before you start packing your bags, let's take a moment to figure out what's best for you – renting or buying? Both have their perks and pitfalls, so let's hash it out.

Renting: More than a Comfy Couch

Alright, first off, let's chat about renting. The major bonus here is flexibility. Get a killer job offer on the other side of the country? No big deal, end your lease, and you're free to go. Plus, if your shower decides to mimic a sprinkler at 2 am, you're not the one to fix it – that's your landlord's job.

But, here's the kicker: you're not the boss. Want to turn your bedroom wall into a mural? Nope. And that monthly rent you're paying? Well, it could rise every year, and it's not helping you build any assets.

Buying: My House, My Rules, but also...My Bills

On the flipside, buying a house is kind of like being king or queen of your own castle. You make the rules. Plus, with each mortgage payment, you're building up equity, which is like a financial building block. And, if you're lucky, your home could increase in value – a definite win.

But here comes the reality check: owning means maintaining. Got a leaky roof? Guess who's got to fix it. And moving isn't as simple as breaking a lease, it's a whole thing. So, make sure you're ready for the commitment.

Money Matters: Mortgages and Down Payments

And now for the million-dollar question – how are you going to pay for your new place? Unless you're a secret billionaire, you're probably looking at getting a mortgage. It's a big loan that you gradually pay off.

Don't forget about the down payment – it's the cash you cough up at the start when you buy a home. The rest of the money? That's where the mortgage comes in.

So, whether you're into the free-spirited life of renting, or you're ready to dive into home ownership, each has its perks and not-so-great bits. And remember, when it comes to financing, mortgages are your friend. Just keep in mind, a bigger down payment can make those monthly payments a little easier to handle.

Real-World Check-In: How They Saved for That Big Purchase

So, we've been yapping about big purchases, saving and budgeting. But hey, let's take a breather and look at how this plays out in the real world. Meet Alex – our resident big-purchase champ who has some experience to share.

The Story of Alex's Wheels

Alex had always dreamt about having a car – a sweet ride that'd make heads turn. But he knew that fancy cars don't just magically appear in driveways, unless you're in a movie, which we're not. He needed a plan, a strategy, a savings game.

He started by setting a budget. After working out his monthly income and expenses, he figured he could set aside a certain amount each month for his car fund. He cut back on takeouts and traded expensive hangouts for budget-friendly fun. Each month, he would squirrel away a portion of his paycheck into a separate savings account just for the car.

Alex was also super smart about picking his car. He had his heart set on a brand new model but knew that a used car would be more within his budget. Sure, it didn't have that new car smell, but it ran smoothly and was in great condition.

The Journey to Car Ownership

The road to car ownership wasn't a sprint; it was more like a marathon. Alex faced some roadblocks. There were months when unexpected expenses cropped up, forcing him to dip into his car savings. But he didn't let these setbacks discourage him. He held on tight to his budget and kept saving.

After about a year, with the combined help of his savings, a trade-in of his old car, and a manageable auto loan, Alex finally bought his own car. The best part? He did it while keeping his finances intact.

Alex's story isn't a tale of overnight success. He didn't find a hidden treasure chest or win the lottery. *Instead, it's a story of planning, sticking to a budget, making smart choices, and being patient.*

When you're planning for your big-ticket items, think of Alex. You don't need a gazillion bucks in the bank. Having a clear plan, staying disciplined, and making mindful decisions will help you. Yeah, it takes some work, but as Alex can tell you, that first drive in his own car? Worth it.

And That's a Wrap: The Lowdown on Large Purchases

Well, you've made it through the whole shebang about planning for large expenses! Now, let's bring it all home and remember the key takeaways.

In this chapter, we've dived into the big, bold world of large purchases like cars and houses. We learned that these are known as 'big-ticket items' and they require some serious planning and saving.

We talked about the pros and cons of buying new versus used cars and learned that while new cars have that fresh-off-the-factory feel and warranty, used cars can offer good value without the high price tag or rapid depreciation.

When it came to houses, we figured out that there's a lot to consider when deciding between renting and buying. Both have their ups and downs, and what works best for you depends on your lifestyle, financial situation, and future plans.

And, of course, we heard about Alex, who gave us a real-world look at what it takes to plan for, save, and finally make a big purchase.

But remember, understanding how to handle money is just part of the journey. The next step is about cultivating a healthy relationship with money itself.

In the next chapter, we'll venture into the mind and explore our attitudes toward money. We'll delve into the idea of 'Money Mindset' and how to foster a positive relationship with your finances. So, strap in and get ready to change how you think and feel about money, because, as we'll discover, your mindset can make a huge difference in achieving your financial goals. So, until then, happy saving and see you in the next chapter!

Chapter 15 - Money Mindset: Cultivating a Positive Relationship with Money

The Importance of a Healthy Money Mindset

H ere's the thing, guys and gals. A money mindset isn't just about numbers, budgets, and bank accounts. It's about your thoughts, feelings, and attitudes towards money. What you believe about money can seriously shape your financial future, more than you might think. No kidding!

Let's play pretend for a moment. Imagine money as a person. Is it a friendly helper, always there when you need a hand? Or is it a tricky villain, always causing problems? Maybe it's a distant stranger, hard to understand, and harder to catch. The way you picture money in your mind can affect the way you handle it in real life.

How Your Money Mindset Impacts Your Financial Health

Now, let's dive a little deeper. Your money mindset is like the captain of your financial ship. It's in the driver's seat, steering your money habits. If you believe that money is hard to come by, you might be super strict with your spending, even to the point where you miss out on fun experiences. On the flip side, if you see money as an unlimited resource, you might splurge a little too often, racking up credit card debt.

Both extremes can be damaging to your financial health. Instead, aiming for a balanced money mindset can help you navigate the tricky waters of finance. That means understanding that money is a tool, not a goal in itself. It means knowing when to save, when to spend, and most importantly, how to do both wisely.

Remember, we're not just talking about how you manage money today. Your money mindset can have long-lasting effects on your life. It can influence how much you save for your future, the type of job you choose, and even how financially secure you feel. So, it's pretty essential to get your money mindset in check.

So, are you ready to take a closer look at your money beliefs and maybe steer your financial ship towards sunnier shores? Let's embark on this voyage together! With the right money mindset, we'll be able to weather any financial storm that comes our way.

Understanding Your Money Beliefs and Where They Come From

What's playing in your head when you think about money? Is it a blockbuster hit or a total flop? In the world of psychology, we call these internal money monologues "money scripts," kind of like the screenplay for your financial life. They're the underlying beliefs that influence how we think, feel, and act around money.

These scripts aren't written overnight. Nope, they develop over time, starting as early as childhood and evolving throughout our lives. The plot twists? They often come from our personal experiences with money – maybe that time you saved up for weeks to buy your first bike, or when you saw a family member struggle with debt. These experiences can leave a lasting imprint on our money mindset.

The Influence of Family and Society on Your Money Beliefs

Now, let's not forget the influence of the people and culture around us. Remember, we don't grow up in a vacuum. Our family, friends, and society at large can all shape our beliefs about money. Think about it. Did your parents chat about finances at the dinner table or was money a hush-hush topic? Do your friends encourage you to save or do they push you to live large?

All these experiences and influences can weave into your money scripts, shaping how you interact with money today. If you grew up hearing that "money is the root of all evil," you might be wary of wealth. If you were always told that "money doesn't grow on trees," you might be super careful about spending.

Case Studies: Examples of Common Money Beliefs and Their Origins

To bring this to life, let's look at some examples. Say you know someone who's always splashing cash, living in the moment with no thought for tomorrow. This might stem from a belief that "you can't take it with you," potentially picked up from a family that prioritized experiences over savings.

Or maybe you've got a friend who never spends a dime without agonizing over it. They could be operating from a money script of scarcity, possibly stemming from a childhood where money was always tight.

Recognizing and understanding these money scripts is the first step to reshaping your money mindset. After all, once you're aware of the screenplay, you can start rewriting it, right? Up next, we'll explore how these money beliefs can impact your financial decisions, and trust me, it's worth sticking around for.

How Your Money Mindset Affects Your Financial Decisions

Money Mindset and Spending Habits: The Connection

Ever caught yourself making it rain on the latest tech or fancy threads while your bestie is all about pinching pennies? Well, it's not just about being a spendthrift or a Scrooge, it's about your money mindset. The way you think about money, like it's a magic carpet ride to happiness or a safety net, heavily influences your spending habits.

How Money Mindset Influences Saving and Investing Decisions

It's not just about your shopping splurges or bargains; your money mindset also shapes how you save and invest. If you're rocking the "money comes and goes" mantra, you might not feel too fussed about having a hefty savings account or trying your hand at the stock market. But if your motto is more "every penny counts," you're likely to be stashing away for the future.

The Role of Money Mindset in Debt and Credit Management

And hey, let's talk about debt and credit cards for a minute. If you see credit cards as a ticket to shop-now-pay-later heaven, you might find yourself with a bigger balance than you'd like. But if you see them as a tool (like a magic wand that needs to be used wisely), you're more likely to clear your dues each month.

Same thing with loans. If you're in the "debt is just a part of life" squad, a student loan or auto loan might not phase you. But if you're in the "debt is a dragon to be slayed" group, you're probably the type to avoid it like a spoiler for your favorite show.

The Impact of a Negative Money Mindset

The Cycle of Financial Stress and Anxiety

Ever found yourself in a sweat thinking about paying bills or checking your bank account? That's financial stress, my friend, and it's a beast that can feed off a negative money mindset. It's like that game of tag where you're "it," but you're just running in circles. The more you stress about money, the more you can slip into a negative mindset, which only fires up more stress. Not the kind of loop you want to be stuck in!

How Negative Money Beliefs Can Lead to Poor Financial Decisions

Just like that catchy song you can't get out of your head, negative money beliefs can sneak into your decision-making process. You might think, "I'll never be able to save enough, so why bother?" or "I'm just bad with money." These kinds of thoughts can lead you to make not-so-great financial choices, like ignoring a growing credit card bill or passing up on a chance to invest.

Real-Life Consequences: Stories of a Negative Money Mindset

Let's talk about Jack. Jack thinks money is something to be feared, and he's always worried he won't have enough. Instead of making a plan to budget and save, he just avoids thinking about it. Over time, his bills pile up, and he winds up in a financial hole that's hard to climb out of.

Then, there's Laura. She's all about living for today, not caring much about tomorrow. But "tomorrow" always comes, right? And for Laura, it comes with a heap of credit card debt from her spur-of-the-moment spending sprees.

Both Jack and Laura are caught in the net of negative money mindsets. They're letting their fear and carelessness dictate their decisions, which only lands them in a tough spot.

So, the bottom line? Negative money mindsets can lead to some real-world messes. The good news? You've got the power to turn it around, and we're here to show you how.

Techniques to Improve Your Money Mindset

Identifying and Challenging Negative Money Beliefs

Got some dark and gloomy thoughts about money swirling around in your head? It's time to call them out, like calling out a bluff in a high-stakes card game. Ask yourself, are you really "bad with money," or are you just not clued up enough about it yet? Challenge these beliefs, throw them out the window, and replace them with ones that actually serve you.

The Power of Affirmations and Visualization for Financial Success

You know that saying, "fake it till you make it"? Yeah, affirmations and visualization work sort of like that. They're all about helping you visualize your goals and speak your success into existence. Try out positive statements like "I've got what it takes to save up for that dream vacation," or "I'm the boss when it comes to making financial decisions." It's like running your own personalized success montage in your mind. Pretty cool, right?

Mindfulness and Money: Techniques for Better Money Management

So, mindfulness might sound like one of those trendy buzzwords, but don't let that fool you. It's the real deal. It's all about being present, about noticing what's going on inside that head of yours without turning it into a judgment fest. And this mindfulness thing? It can totally transform how you handle your money. You'll start thinking twice before smashing that "buy now" button or deciding to tuck away some cash instead of spending it on a whim. You could try out some mindfulness exercises like deep breathing or even meditation to help keep you grounded when dealing with your money.

But, let's be real, changing how you think about money isn't something that's going to happen overnight. It's like trying to perfect that dance move that's been trending on social media: it takes time, patience, and a whole lot of practice. But keep at it, and before you know it, you'll have turned your money mindset around. And that means a healthier relationship with your money and a future that's looking way brighter. Now, that's what we're aiming for!

The Power of a Positive Money Mindset

The Benefits of Cultivating a Positive Relationship with Money

Look, you and money are going to be lifelong partners, so you might as well make the relationship a good one, right? Kind of like turning an annoying sibling rivalry into a super cool friendship. Cultivating a positive money mindset doesn't just help you with all the numbers stuff, it's also great for your overall well-being. Imagine feeling less stressed about bills, or knowing that you've got enough cash set aside for that new gaming console or those must-have concert tickets. That's what a positive money mindset can do for you.

Committing to Ongoing Money Mindset Work: It's a Journey, Not a Destination

Here's the thing, though, working on your money mindset is more of a marathon, not a sprint. It's not about making quick changes and expecting instant results. It's an ongoing journey, kind of like your favorite long-running TV show. You stick with it because you're invested in the characters and you want to see how the plot unfolds. And like the best TV shows, there might be twists and turns, but the end result is so worth it.

When you commit to improving your money mindset, you're investing in yourself. And that's the best investment you could ever make. So why not start today? Start small, make it a habit, and keep going. Because when it comes to your money mindset, the power is totally in your hands. It's like holding the controller when you're playing your favorite video game. You get to decide what happens next. And that's an exciting place to be!

And remember, you're not alone. There's a whole community of people just like you who are working to improve their money mindset. So, keep going, stay positive, and remember, every step you take on this journey is a step towards a more financially healthy and confident you.

Now it's time to show the world (and your bank account) what you're made of.

Ready, Set, Recall

Alright! You've just worked your way through an expansive journey discussing plans and financing for your future. It's time to pause and reflect on the wealth of knowledge you've collected. Get ready for your quiz! It's a fantastic way to assess your understanding and strengthen your grasp of the topics. There are 17 questions in this quiz. Remember, it's not about getting everything perfect - it's about reinforcing your learning and preparing yourself for a financially secure future! Answers can be found in the Resources chapter at the end of the book.

Now, let's get started!

1. What are student loans?
    a) A type of personal loan
    b) Money given by your school to cover tuition
    c) Funds you borrow to pay for higher education
    d) Money awarded for academic achievement

2. What's the difference between a scholarship and a grant?
    a) Scholarships need to be repaid, grants don't
    b) Grants are based on financial need, scholarships on merit
    c) Scholarships are given by the government, grants by private organizations
    d) There is no difference, both terms mean the same thing

3. When it comes to student loans, how should you decide how much to borrow?

a) Always borrow the maximum amount

b) Only borrow what you need to cover tuition

c) Borrow enough to live comfortably during your years at school

d) Consider your future earning potential, living expenses, and tuition costs

4. Why is it important to start retirement planning early?

a) To maximize compound interest

b) You need to start early to qualify for Social Security

c) Retirement planning can't be done later in life

d) Retirement planning is mandatory at a certain age

5.Which of the following is NOT a type of retirement account?

a) Roth IRA

b) 401(k)

c) Certificate of Deposit (CD)

d) Traditional IRA

6. How does Social Security work?

a) It's a mandatory savings account for every worker

b) It's a program where workers earn credits for retirement benefits

c) It's a private insurance program

d) It's a retirement plan offered by employers

7. Which of the following is NOT a retirement risk

a) Inflation

b) Longevity

c) Investment performance

d) Excessive savings

8. What's the difference between buying a new car and a used car?

a) A new car is always a better option

b) A used car is always a better option

c) A new car depreciates faster but comes with a warranty, a used car costs less upfront but may have higher maintenance costs

    d) There's no difference in the long run

9. What factors should you consider in the rent vs. buy debate?

    a) Whether you can afford the down payment on a house

    b) If you plan to move in the next few years

    c) Your financial stability and readiness to take on the responsibility of home ownership

    d) All of the above

10. What is a money mindset?

    a) Your beliefs and attitudes about money

    b) The amount of money you have in the bank

    c) A type of savings account

    d) Your spending habits

11. Where do your money beliefs come from?

    a) Your parents

    b) Your experiences

    c) Society and culture

    d) All of the above

12. How can a negative money mindset affect you?

    a) It can prevent you from making good financial decisions

    b) It doesn't affect your financial choices

    c) It can lead to an increase in wealth

    d) It can make you more

13. Which of the following is a technique to improve your money mindset?

    a) Practicing gratitude

    b) Reading financial news daily

    c) Spending money impulsively

    d) Ignoring your bank statements

14. What are the benefits of a positive money mindset?
    a) It can improve your financial decisions
    b) It can lead to increased wealth
    c) It can lead to a better understanding of financial matters
    d) All of the above

15. When planning for large expenses, what is a key consideration?
    a) Your current income level
    b) Your savings strategy and timeline
    c) The brand of the product you are purchasing
    d) The opinion of friends and family

16. What is the purpose of cultivating a positive relationship with money?
    a) To ensure you are the richest person in your social circle
    b) To alleviate stress and bring more joy into your life
    c) To ensure you never have to think about money again
    d) To impress others with your wealth

17. How do pensions and employer-sponsored retirement plans contribute to retirement planning?
    a) They are mandatory and everyone must participate
    b) They supplement Social Security and personal savings, providing additional income during retirement
    c) They are the only way to save for retirement
    d) They don't contribute to retirement planning

VI

Part 6 - Investing

Chapter 16 - The Exciting World of Investing: An Intro

Alright, so you've got your money in order, you've learned about saving, and you've mastered budgeting. But where do you go from here? Welcome to the exciting world of investing! This isn't just for Wall Street tycoons or those dudes in fancy suits. It's a key tool for building wealth, and it's totally accessible, even for us everyday folks.

Stocks 101: Your Piece of the Corporate Pie

Stocks are your golden ticket to owning a piece of your favorite companies. It's like being part owner of a super cool treehouse...only, this one's a multi-billion dollar business.

So, What's a Stock?

Here's the deal: when you buy a stock, you're buying a teeny, tiny slice of a company. Imagine the company as a giant pizza; every stock is a delicious, money-filled slice. When the company rakes in the cash, your slice gets a bit tastier. But if the company's struggling, your slice might not be so yummy.

Stocks: The High-Risk, High-Reward Game

Stocks are a bit like the adrenaline junkies of the investment world. Their values can bounce up and down faster than your favorite catchy pop song. But that's what makes them exciting. They're risky, sure, but they can also give you hefty returns. Think about it: higher risk often comes with the chance of higher reward.

Owning a Fraction of a Fraction?

Now here's something awesome: you don't need to be a billionaire to buy stocks. In fact, you can buy just a fraction of a stock, thanks to something cool called fractional shares. That means you can get in on the action, even if some of those big-name stocks seem way too pricey.

Brace Yourself for the Stock Coaster

Stocks can take you on a wild ride, no doubt about that. Their values can be up one day, down the next. But don't let that freak you out. It's all part of the thrill of the stock market. If you're in it for the long game, these short-term thrills are just part of the journey.

Remember, stocks are just one type of investment. They can be super powerful, but balance is key. Think of it like a healthy diet—you wouldn't only eat pizza, right? Don't worry, we'll get into more of that balance talk later.

Bonds: Be the Banker, Earn Interest

Now let's cruise down another investment avenue - bonds. Bonds are less of a roller coaster and more of a leisurely drive. They're considered safer than stocks, but the trade-off is the return might not be as sky-high.

What's a Bond, Anyway?

Think of bonds as being the bank in a loan transaction. When you buy a bond, you're lending your hard-earned money to a company, city, or even the government. It's like saying, "Hey, I'll lend you some of my cash, but you've got to pay me back with a little extra for my troubles." That 'little extra' is the interest you earn.

Safety First: Why Bonds Are Less Risky

Bonds are like the designated drivers of the investment world. They're considered safer because the issuer has a legal obligation to pay you back. It's not a pinky promise; it's a legally binding agreement. If a company goes belly-up, bondholders are typically paid back before stockholders. So, in the financial equivalent of a sinking ship, owning a bond is like having a spot on a lifeboat.

But...Lower Returns?

Remember the saying, "No risk, no reward?" Well, it applies here. Bonds are generally less risky than stocks, but that safety comes at a cost: lower potential returns. It's like choosing a steady job over a start-up. The start-up (like a stock) could make you rich, or it could flop. A steady job (like a bond) might not make you a millionaire, but it offers stability and a regular paycheck.

Bonds may not be as flashy as stocks, but they're a key ingredient in your investment mix. They provide a stable foundation that can help keep your financial goals on track, even when the stock market gets a little wild.

Funds: It's Like an Investment Buffet!

Now that we've got the basics of stocks and bonds under our belt, let's jump into another investment category - funds. Mutual funds, index funds, exchange-traded funds - they're all on the menu at this investment buffet.

What's a Fund?

Okay, imagine you and your friends want to buy a pizza, but everyone likes different toppings. Instead of each person buying a whole pizza, you all chip in and get a variety pack - everyone gets a slice of what they want. That's sort of what a fund is in the investing world.

When you buy a fund, you're not just buying a single stock or bond; you're buying a slice of a big investment pizza. That 'pizza' could have a bit of this company's stock, a bit of that company's bond, and a slice of another investment - all in one convenient package.

Different Flavors: Mutual Funds, Index Funds, and ETFs

There are a few different types of funds, each with their own flavor.

Mutual funds are like ordering a pizza with your friends. You all chip in, and a professional money manager decides how to divide the money among different stocks and bonds to make the best portfolio!

Index funds are a bit different. Instead of a money manager deciding on the mix, index funds aim to mimic a specific index - like the S&P 500. It's like ordering a pre-set pizza combo.

Exchange-traded funds, or ETFs, are a hybrid. They can be traded like individual stocks but represent a collection of investments, like a mutual fund or an index fund.

In short, funds offer a way to invest in a wide array of stocks, bonds, and other investments - all in one go. They're a handy tool to have in your investment toolbox!

Real Estate: Not Just Home Sweet Home

Let's switch gears and chat about real estate, the kind of investment you can actually touch and feel.

Money-Making Mansions

We're talking about putting your dollars into bricks and mortar — properties like houses, apartments, or even commercial buildings. Investing in real estate gives you a unique and concrete asset, something you can stand on, touch, or renovate. The real kick is, it can be a savvy way to grow your wealth.

Two Paths to Property Profits

If you're interested in real estate, you've got a couple of options. One route is to buy a property and then rent it out. Think about it like this: You get a house or an apartment, and then someone else pays you rent to live there. Sweet deal, right? The money you rake in from the rent could help you pay off any loan you may have taken out to buy the property. Over time, you'll own the property outright, and the rent you've collected has done a chunk of the hard work for you.

If buying an entire property sounds a bit ambitious right now, don't sweat it. There's another way in: Real Estate Investment Trusts, or REITs for short. These are a bit like mutual funds, but instead of dealing with stocks or bonds, they're all about real estate. They gather up money from a bunch of investors (like yourself) to buy and manage properties. The awesome part is you can buy and sell shares of a REIT as easily as trading stocks.

With Property Power Comes Property Responsibility

But remember, becoming a property investor isn't all about counting your cash. With property comes responsibility. Think maintenance, taxes, and sometimes managing tenants. It's not always a walk in the park. Yet, with some good research and smart decisions, real estate could be a seriously profitable part of your wealth-building strategy. You never know, you might just be the next property mogul!

Time Value of Money: Compound Interest, Your Best Friend

Imagine if your money could multiply on its own. Pretty cool, right? Welcome to the concept of compound interest, a superpower in the world of finance.

Compound interest is basically earning interest on interest. So, say you invest some money and make a profit. Next time around, you earn a profit on your original investment AND the profit you made. And then you do it again, and again, and... well, you get the point. Over time, your wealth can start to snowball, getting bigger and bigger as the years roll by.

But here's the kicker: time is of the essence. The longer you let your money do its thing, the bigger that snowball can get. That's the time value of money, folks. Money today is worth more than the same amount in the future because of its potential to grow over time.

We covered this concept in more detail in chapter 8, so if you're curious to know more, make sure to head on over for a refresher.

Balance Act: Risk vs Reward

Now, I won't sugarcoat it. Investing is not a guaranteed path to quick riches. It's all about balancing risk and reward. You've probably heard the saying, "no risk, no reward," right? It's especially true when it comes to investing.

In general, investments with the potential for higher returns also come with a higher risk. Stocks, for instance, could give you hefty returns if the company does well. But, there's also the chance the company might not perform as expected, which could lead to losses.

On the other hand, investments like bonds are generally considered safer, but the returns are usually not as high. So, you gotta figure out what balance works for you and your goals.

Diversification: Don't Put All Your Eggs in One Basket

Here's a pro tip for managing risk: diversification. Ever heard the phrase "don't put all your eggs in one basket?" It's a pretty solid piece of advice when it comes to investing.

Diversification is about spreading your money across different types of investments. Think stocks, bonds, funds, real estate, and even retirement accounts and cryptocurrencies. The idea is that if one investment doesn't do so hot, others might do well, which can help balance out any losses.

So, remember: investing is about the long game, balancing risk and reward, and spreading out your investments. Keep these concepts in mind as you navigate the investing world, and you'll be well on your way to building wealth

Choosing the Right Mix: Your Financial Recipe

Now you've got a destination in mind, how do you get there? This part's all about creating your investment recipe – a.k.a. your asset allocation.

Each type of investment, whether it's stocks, bonds, funds, or real estate, brings something different to your financial table. Your mission? To find a blend that matches your goals, risk comfort level, and time frame. It's about finding a sweet spot that pushes your money to work harder without causing you endless sleepless nights.

Regular Review and Rebalancing: Your Financial Health Check-ups

Alright, goals are set, the asset mix is sorted, and you're off investing – awesome! But hold up a sec, you're not done. Investments are like houseplants. They need regular check-ups and a bit of TLC.

The fancy term for this is rebalancing. It's all about making sure your portfolio stays on the right track, aligned with your financial goals. Investments can grow at different rates, and without regular check-ups, your carefully selected mix could get out of balance. So, keep an eye on your financial greenery and don't be afraid to prune and tweak as needed.

Using Apps and Technology: Investing in the 21st Century

Thanks to the wonders of technology, you've got a whole host of apps and platforms to help you stay on top of your investing game. Apps like Robinhood, Acorns, and Betterment are like your digital financial assistants, ready to help you track, rebalance, and automate your investing process.

Crafting an investment plan and monitoring your portfolio may seem like a tall order, but with clear goals, the right mix, regular check-ups, and some tech-savvy tools, you'll be bossing your financial future in no time.

We've linked the tools we mentioned and some more that we use ourselves in the resources chapter at the end of the book.

So, what's next, you ask? We're about to level up, that's what! We've covered the whats and whys of investing, and now it's time to tackle the hows. How can you make your money grow without taking crazy risks? How do the real big players in investing win their game? How can you turn all this learning into action?

So get ready for the next thrill ride! We're about to move from the basics of investing to some serious strategy talk. The next chapter is all about arming you with some wickedly effective tips and tactics that could totally change your game in the world of investing. Stay with us, because we're just getting warmed up!

Chapter 17 - Successful Investing Tips and Strategies

Alright, gather 'round, folks! In this chapter, we're going to break down some insider secrets of successful investing – think of it as cracking the code to that treasure chest. We'll explore the power of regular investing and why staying chill, even when the market's throwing a tantrum, is key.

We're also going to peek under the hood of some potential investments and decipher financial health checks like a pro. Last but definitely not least, we'll check out when you might want to tag in a financial advisor to join your quest and how to pick the right one.

Buckle up, future millionaires. Let's get this show on the road!

Consistent Investing: Your Ticket to the Wealth Club

Let's take a minute to talk about the real-life story of Tim, a regular guy with a superpower - patience. Tim was just a regular teen like you, with an allowance that wasn't anything to write home about. But Tim had a brainwave one day. He decided he'd start investing a little bit of his money consistently, every single month, into the stock market. Rain or shine, bull market or bear, Tim was out there, investing like clockwork.

Fast forward a few years, and Tim's buddies are scrambling to pay off student loans and buy their first cars, while Tim? Tim's looking at a seriously impressive pile of dough in his investment account, all thanks to the magic of consistent investing.

So, what's the secret sauce here? It's a sweet little trick called dollar-cost averaging. Now, that might sound like something your math teacher would drone on about, but don't hit snooze just yet. Dollar-cost averaging is just a cool way of saying that you're putting the same amount of money into your investments, consistently, no matter what Wall Street's mood is.

Think of it like a diet - but a fun one. Instead of stuffing yourself on payday and then starving for the rest of the month, you're eating a little bit every day. And the best part? When the market gets gloomy and prices drop, you get more shares for your buck. And when it picks up again? You're already holding the winning ticket.

So, folks, let's take a leaf out of Tim's book. Consistent investing isn't about making a quick buck. It's the slow and steady race to a future where you're the boss of your own wealth. After all, even the smallest drops can fill a mighty ocean over time, right? Just ask Tim!

Emotional Discipline: Keep Your Cool, Folks

Okay, let's pivot to something we don't talk about enough - emotional discipline. I'm not talking about some deep meditation technique or yoga pose here. We're talking about keeping your head cool, especially when the stock market starts acting like a season finale of your favorite drama series.

You know how it is, right? One day the market's chill, and the next day it's freaking out like it just saw a ghost. But just like we shouldn't take every plot twist in our favorite show too seriously, we shouldn't overreact to every single bump and dip in the market.

Now, picture this: The market's on a downward slide, and you're starting to panic. You might feel like that character who, at the first hint of trouble, decides to pack up and move to a different city. But in reality, you'd just be making a rash decision based on the heat of the moment. And trust me, that rarely ends well.

Instead, aim to be that cool character who keeps their wits about them, even when things get crazy. They're not trying to outsmart the plot twists or leave town. They're sticking it out, making thoughtful choices, and, more often than not, coming out on top.

Remember, no one can predict every twist and turn the market's going to throw at us, just like no one can predict the next shocking scene in our favorite drama series. Dancing in and out of the market based on emotions is about as sensible as trying to choreograph a dance routine in the middle of a hurricane - you're just going to end up disoriented and soaking wet.

So, keep your popcorn ready for the market's drama, but don't let it sway you from your investment game. Just sit back, enjoy the show, and remember - it's just a show. Your real success comes from keeping your cool and playing your game, not getting sucked into the market's drama.

Long-term Perspective: It's a Marathon, Not a Sprint

Let's wrap this up by talking about the long-term perspective. Imagine you're going on a road trip. You wouldn't turn back just because you hit a speed bump or a pothole, right? It's the same with investing. Short-term ups and downs are like those speed bumps and potholes.

It's essential to keep your eyes on the prize and stay invested for the long haul. Your investment ride might get bumpy at times, but remember, you're in this for the long, scenic journey. It's all about letting your money grow over time.

Regular investing, emotional discipline, and a long-term perspective - three ingredients for a potent wealth-building recipe. And remember, every great investor started with these basics. So, strap in, keep calm, and invest on.

The Scoop on Researching Potential Investments

Financial Statements: The "Big Three" You Need to Know

Alright, so financial statements. Maybe not the most glamorous topic, but stick with me here. Let's reimagine these financial statements as members of a championship basketball team - the point guard, the center, and the shooting guard. Each plays a different but key role in winning the game, just like the balance sheet, income statement, and cash flow statement do for a company.

The balance sheet, that's your point guard - the strategic playmaker. It's running the game, giving you a snapshot of a company's assets (what it owns) and liabilities (what it owes). It's your game overview at any given moment.

Next up, the income statement - this is your center, the powerhouse. Like a center who's all about scoring points and defending, the income statement details the company's revenues (points scored) and expenses (points conceded). This is your play-by-play of the company's performance over time.

Lastly, we've got the cash flow statement - the elusive shooting guard. Just like a shooting guard that can swiftly change the game's direction, the cash flow statement helps you track the company's cash sources and usage, showing how it maneuvers its financial resources.

So, when you're figuring out a company's financial health, just think - point guard, center, and shooting guard. It'll help you determine if a company is a financial championship contender or if it's just a beginner on the court.

Financial Ratios: Company Health in a Nutshell

Up next, we're delving into the less-explored but incredibly awesome terrain of financial ratios. Sounds fancy, doesn't it? Well, it's simpler than it sounds, and let's be honest, it's pretty cool too.

Think of financial ratios as your special decoder glasses that help you see the financial health of a company in 4K UHD clarity. They're like your secret weapon in understanding these key aspects of a company: profitability, liquidity, and leverage. Scared of big words? No worries, we're going to break them down for you.

1. **Profitability**: This is about the big bucks, the cash flow. In simple terms, how much money is the company making after all expenses are paid? If they're raking in the dough, that's a good sign. It's like checking the stats of a basketball player: more points mean better performance.

2. **Liquidity**: You know how in video games, the character always needs enough potions to survive battles? Well, in the finance world, liquidity is those potions. It's about whether the company has enough resources (read: cash) to cover its short-term debts. You don't want your company running out of potions in the middle of the game, do you?

3. **Leverage**: This is all about the company's debt diet. How much debt does the company have compared to its assets or equity? A company with too much debt might be like a Jenga tower, one wrong move and it can all come tumbling down. But remember, just like some level of difficulty makes video games fun, some level of debt is necessary for a company to grow and expand.

Remember, you don't need to be a maths prodigy to get these ratios. They're here to simplify the financial jargon and give you a way to compare companies as easily as picking your favorite among the Avengers.

So, pull out your decoder glasses, fellow finance adventurer! It's time to crack the code and get a crystal clear picture of where to drop your hard-earned coins. Your journey to becoming a master of money is just getting started!

Beyond Numbers: The Story Beneath the Figures

You see, a company isn't merely an assembly of statistics; it's a thrilling narrative that unfolds over time. The digits and decimals only give you part of the story. For the real scoop, you have to dig a little deeper. Like an adventurous archaeologist uncovering hidden secrets, you have to look at the competitive landscape, analyze the top honchos, and keep an eye out for industry-shaking trends. These aren't just trivia but the keys to unlocking a treasure chest of smart investments.

So, in the quest to hunt down the best investments, think of yourself as a finance archaeologist. Your task? To explore the ruins of financial statements, decipher the hieroglyphs of market trends, and unearth the hidden treasure of a promising investment. The artifacts you seek aren't ancient pottery or lost scrolls but valuable insights that help you predict where the investment winds are blowing.

Remember, in the thrilling adventure of investment, your mission is to find the best place to stash your loot for bountiful returns.

Alright, investment trailblazers! We've made it. We've journeyed through the terrain of financial statements, dodged the quicksands of market roller coasters, and bravely ventured into the intriguing underworld of company narratives. From deciphering the mysterious symbols of balance sheets to cultivating the courage to stay calm in the face of market mood swings, you've come a long way from where we began.

But remember, no explorer's pack is complete without a good map. In our case, that map is a mix of figures, trends, financial records, and a dash of human instinct. Understanding this map, navigating the investment landscape, and charting a course that's right for you, is what this journey's been all about. So, keep doing your financial digging, and continue unearthing those nuggets of investment wisdom.

Now, it's time to test your knowledge, to see if you're ready to navigate the wild terrain of the investing world on your own. The next leg? A quiz to recap all the things we've learnt in this part of the book.

Before we dive into that, remember this: Investing isn't just about making money. It's about learning, growing, and yes, a bit of thrill-seeking. You've begun your ride into this exhilarating world, and this is just the start.

Ready, Set, Recall

Hey, super saver! We've traveled quite a distance in our financial journey, and now it's time to reflect on what we've discovered in this section. Don't fret if you don't ace it in the first go. This is all about helping you recall the key points and to strengthen your money management muscle. So take a deep breath, tap into your memory bank, and let's see how much you've absorbed from the fascinating world of investing!

1. What is a stock?
   a) A type of soup
   b) A piece of ownership in a company
   c) A type of bond
   d) A special type of bank account

2. What does it mean to diversify your investments?
   a) Put all your money into one investment
   b) Spread your investments across various types of assets
   c) Only invest in stocks
   d) Only invest in bonds

3. What is the time value of money concept in relation to investing?
   a) Money is more valuable the longer you hold onto it
   b) Money decreases in value over time due to inflation
   c) The idea that money available now is worth more than the same amount

in the future because of its potential earning capacity

    d) Money can't buy happiness

4. What is a bond in the context of investing?

    a) A type of insurance policy

    b) A loan made to a company or government

    c) An ownership share in a company

    d) A physical object that is worth money

5. What is a fund in the context of investing?

    a) A savings account

    b) A collection of investments, such as stocks or bonds

    c) A type of loan

    d) An agreement between two parties

6. How can emotional discipline contribute to successful investing?

    a) It can help you avoid making impulsive decisions based on short-term market fluctuations

    b) It ensures that you always buy high and sell low

    c) It helps you predict the future performance of the stock market

    d) It ensures that you always follow the advice of friends and family when investing

7. What is the benefit of regular investing?

    a) It allows you to predict the future performance of your investments

    b) It reduces the risk of your investments

    c) It takes advantage of dollar-cost averaging, which can lower the average cost per share of an investment

    d) It ensures that you always make money from your investments

8. What does the "drummer" - the cash flow statement - in the financial statement band analogy reveal about a company?

    a) The amount of debts the company has to pay

b) The revenue and expenses of the company

c) The financial status of the company including its assets and liabilities

d) Where the company's cash is coming from and where it's being used

9. What is the concept of risk versus reward in investing?

a) The idea that investments with higher risk tend to offer higher potential returns

b) The notion that all investments are risky and therefore not worthwhile

c) The belief that only high-risk investments are worth considering

d) The concept that low-risk investments always provide the highest returns

10. What is real estate investing?

a) Investing in stocks and bonds only

b) The process of buying, owning, managing, renting, or selling real estate for profit

c) The practice of buying expensive properties to show off

d) Buying as many properties as possible, regardless of the cost

VII

Part 7 - Money Survival Guide: Contracts, Insurance, and Beating Fraudsters at Their Game

Chapter 18 - Understanding Contracts and Insurance Basics

H ave you ever clicked on that "I Agree" button when signing up for an app or setting up a new device? If yes, congratulations, you've engaged with a contract. Ever heard your parents talk about auto insurance or health insurance? Yup, that's another big part of our adult lives. So, welcome to the exciting world of contracts and insurance!

Alright, we know it might not sound like the most thrilling topic at first. But imagine buying your first car, signing up for a cool new app, or renting your first apartment. All these scenarios involve contracts, and guess what? Insurance is often not far behind.

You see, understanding contracts and insurance is kind of like learning a secret language. It helps you navigate the world of adulthood with more confidence. Plus, it can save you a lot of stress (and money!) in the long run. And who wouldn't like a little more of that in their life, right?

Let's take a look at a couple of examples. Say you're signing up for a new music streaming app. They've got all your favorite artists, and they're offering a free trial. Sweet, right? You quickly scroll through the terms and conditions and hit "I Agree." Boom - you've just entered into a contract. And that tiny print you skipped over? It's packed with important details about what you can do with your music, what the app can do with your data, and what happens after the free trial ends. Knowing how to navigate that fine print can make all the difference between enjoying your tunes trouble-free and getting hit with unexpected charges or data privacy issues.

And how about insurance? Think about your dream car. You've been saving for it, and it's finally yours. As exciting as this is, it also comes with new responsibilities, like getting auto insurance. Knowing the basics of how insurance works can help you pick the right policy, understand what it covers, and even save a couple of bucks on premiums.

These are just a few ways understanding contracts and insurance can affect our daily lives. But fear not, we're about to dive in and break it all down. So buckle up and let's get started!

Decoding Contracts

You might be wondering what a contract actually is. Does it have to be a ten-page document filled with complicated words? Or can it just be an agreement between two friends? Let's dig in.

What is a Contract?

In the simplest terms, a contract is an agreement between two or more parties. It sets out what everyone has agreed to do (or not do), and can be in writing or sometimes even verbal (although written contracts are way easier to prove if things get messy). Contracts are a big deal because they form the basis for tons of interactions in our lives - from buying a car to signing up for a new app on your phone.

But why are they so important? Well, contracts help to make sure everyone knows what's expected of them. They're like the rulebook for the agreement.

If someone doesn't stick to their side of the deal, the contract can be used to help sort things out. So knowing your way around a contract is a super useful life skill.

Common Types of Contracts

As a teenager, there are a few types of contracts that you're likely to come across more often. Let's take a closer look at some of these:

Mobile Phone Contracts: Ever wondered what you're agreeing to when you get a new phone plan? These contracts set out everything from how many minutes and data you get each month, to what happens if you want to end the plan early.

Rental Agreements: Thinking about moving into your first apartment or renting a room near your college? Rental agreements set out the details about how much rent you need to pay, when it's due, and what you need to do to get your deposit back when you move out.

Understanding Online Contracts and Terms of Service: Every time you sign up for a new app or online service, you're entering into a contract. These are often called 'Terms of Service' or 'User Agreements,' and they cover stuff like how your personal data is used and what you can and can't do on the platform.

Reading a Contract: What to Look For

Ok, so we know contracts are important, but they can also be kind of intimidating. All that legal jargon and tiny print - where do you even start? Well, here are a few things to look out for when you're reading a contract:

- **The Parties:** This is who the contract is between. Make sure your name is spelled correctly!

- **The Terms:** These are the details of what each party is agreeing to. Make sure you understand what you're signing up for.

- **The Duration:** How long is the contract for? Is it a one-off thing, or does it last for a certain period of time?

- **The Fine Print:** Sometimes important details are hidden away in smaller print. Keep an eye out for anything that talks about extra fees, what happens if something goes wrong, or how to end the contract.

Remember, it's totally okay to take your time and ask questions if there's something you don't understand. A contract is a big commitment, and it's important to know what you're getting into. After all, knowledge is power, especially when it comes to your rights and responsibilities.

Introduction to Insurance

Alright, so now that we've got the hang of contracts, let's dive into the fascinating world of insurance. No, really, stick with me here. While it might not sound like the most thrilling topic, understanding insurance can seriously come in handy. It's like having a safety net for the unexpected surprises life loves to throw our way.

What is Insurance?

In a nutshell, insurance is a way of protecting yourself against financial loss.

It's a contract (yes, another one of those!) where you pay a company a regular amount of money - called a premium - and in return, they promise to cover certain types of losses if they happen.

The key here is the word "if." Unlike your Netflix subscription where you pay and get something every month, with insurance, you're paying for the "just in case." You hope you won't need to use it, but if something unexpected does happen, like a car accident or a serious illness, insurance can help cover the costs.

Common Types of Insurance

There are many types of insurance out there, but let's break down some of the big ones that you'll likely come across:

Auto Insurance: If you're a driver, this one's a must. It can help cover costs if you're in a car accident, if your car gets damaged, or even if it gets stolen. Plus, it's legally required in most places.

Health Insurance: Nobody plans to get sick or hurt, but when it does happen, medical costs can add up quick. Health insurance can help cover those costs, from regular check-ups to emergency room visits and everything in between.

Life Insurance: This one's a bit morbid to think about, but life insurance can provide money to your loved ones if you were to pass away. It's especially important if you have people who depend on your income.

Homeowner's or Renter's Insurance: Whether you own your place or are renting, insurance can help protect you from the costs of damage to your home or belongings from things like fire, theft, or even a burst pipe.

How Insurance Works

So, we've got these different types of insurance, but how do they actually work? Well, it all comes down to a few key concepts:

- **Premiums:** This is the amount you pay to the insurance company, usually every month. The cost of your premium depends on a bunch of different things, like your age, health, and the type of coverage you want.

- **Deductibles:** This is the amount you have to pay out of your own pocket before the insurance company starts to pay. For example, if you have a $500 deductible on your car insurance, and you have a fender bender that costs $2,000, you'd pay the first $500 and the insurance company would pay the remaining $1,500.

- **Coverage:** This is what the insurance company agrees to pay for. Each insurance policy has different coverage, so it's important to read the details and know what's included.

- **Claims:** If you have a loss that's covered by your insurance, you file a claim. This is basically asking the insurance company to pay for the loss according to your coverage.

In essence, insurance is all about managing risk. It's like a backup plan for when things don't go as planned. Remember, while you can't predict the future, with a bit of knowledge and planning, you can certainly prepare for it.

Interplay of Contracts and Insurance

It's time to bring our two big topics together – contracts and insurance. They may seem like completely separate ideas, but in reality, they often work hand in hand. They complement each other in ways that make the business and legal world go 'round.

How Contracts and Insurance Often Go Hand-in-Hand

Think about it this way - contracts are all about setting terms, conditions, and promises between parties. Meanwhile, insurance is a way to ensure that money won't be a problem if something happens and you need to fulfill those promises.

For example, let's say you have a contract with a phone company. Your agreement could state that if you accidentally break your phone, you'll have to pay a hefty fee. But if you've got insurance on your phone (which is another contract, by the way), the insurance company promises to cover the cost of a new phone or repairs. So in this case, having an insurance contract helps you fulfill your original phone contract.

Examples of Contracts That Require Insurance

There are many contracts out there that require you to have some sort of insurance. This is because the other party wants to make sure that if something goes wrong, there'll be enough money to cover the losses. It's like their own way of managing risk.

Car Leases or Loans: If you lease or finance a car, the contract will require you to have auto insurance. This isn't just because it's the law in most places. It's also because the finance company wants to make sure they won't be left hanging if you get into an accident and can't make the payments.

Rental Agreements: Landlords often require tenants to have renter's insurance. This is to protect their property in case of damages, but it also benefits you. It can help cover the cost of your belongings if there's a fire, theft, or other kinds of damage.

This mingling of contracts and insurance is a classic dance you'll see in many parts of life. Understanding how they work together can give you a serious edge when you're navigating adult responsibilities.

From the nitty-gritty of contracts to the complexities of insurance, we've unlocked some essential life skills. Skills that not only make you more prepared for the adult world but also might save you a bunch of stress and money in the long run.

Here's the thing, though. Knowing about this stuff isn't enough. It's essential to put it into action. Don't be the person who just scrolls to the bottom and clicks "I agree" without reading the terms. Be the person who knows what they're signing up for.

And when it comes to insurance, don't just opt out because it seems like an extra cost. Think about what you stand to lose and whether insurance might be a smart way to protect yourself.

Call to Action: Review a Contract in Their Life with Newfound Understanding

Here's a challenge for you: find a contract in your life – maybe it's for your mobile phone, a game you downloaded, or even your parents' rental agreement or car insurance policy. Take some time to go through it with your newfound understanding. See what you can decipher and what questions come up.

But wait, don't let your guard down just yet. Even if you've become a contract wizard and an insurance guru, there are still some mischievous villains lurking in the shadows that you need to be aware of. It's like a plot twist in your favorite superhero movie.

Imagine this, you've built a fortress of financial security with well-negotiated contracts and smart insurance decisions. Now, you have to protect this fortress from the sly invaders like fraudsters and identity thieves. Sounds like a serious spy movie mission, doesn't it?

So, in the next chapter, we'll uncover the sneaky tactics of these financial tricksters and arm you with strategies to outsmart them. Gear up for Chapter 19 - "Keeping Your Finances Safe: Preventing Fraud and Identity Theft," where we'll master the art of financial self-defense.

Chapter 19 - Keeping Your Finances Safe: Preventing Fraud and Identity Theft

W e're living in a world that's more connected than ever before, where the swipe of a finger or a couple of taps on a screen can get us food, clothes, and even a ride home. While all of this is pretty cool, it's also pretty risky. Enter the world of fraud and identity theft. Unsettling as it is, these things are as much a part of our digital age as the latest TikTok dance or meme format.

You might be wondering, "Fraud and identity theft, are they that common?" The answer is a resounding yes! These aren't just plotlines for crime dramas on Netflix. They're real, they're happening, and they're more widespread than you might think. Every year, millions of people worldwide fall victim to these acts, suffering financial losses and the nightmarish task of setting their lives back in order.

The impact of fraud and identity theft can be enormous. Imagine one day, you're chillin' at home, the next, you get a call about a loan you never took or a credit card bill for a shopping spree you didn't enjoy. Sounds scary, right? That's because it is. Your hard-earned money, your credit score, even your reputation - they're all at risk.

But, don't panic! While the risks are real, so are the ways to protect yourself. It's all about being vigilant, staying informed, and taking proactive steps to guard against these threats. Because remember, in this digital world, your personal information is as valuable as gold and needs to be protected like it.

So, grab a comfy seat and maybe a snack, because we're about to deep-dive into understanding fraud and identity theft, how to spot them, and more importantly, how to guard against them. The more you know, the better you can protect yourself, and that's what it's all about, right?

Understanding Fraud

Before we dive in, let's get our heads around what fraud is. Think of it like someone telling a big fat lie or putting up an act, but instead of winning an Oscar, they're trying to snatch away your money or valuables. In more formal terms, fraud is any deceptive act meant to result in financial or personal gain.

There are several types of fraud, each as sneaky and damaging as the next. We'll dive into a few big ones.

First off, credit card fraud. Picture this: you're out enjoying a day with friends, and when you reach for your card to pay for your avocado toast, it's gone. Freaky, right? Now, imagine someone else is living it up on your dime. Even freakier. Credit card fraud happens when someone uses your card (or just the card information) to make unauthorized purchases.

Then there's bank fraud, which happens when someone uses sneaky tricks to empty out your bank account or open an account in your name without your permission. It's like they're playing a real twisted version of Monopoly with your life savings.

Internet fraud is another big one in this digital age. This involves any scam that uses the internet - email scams, phishing, online shopping scams. You name it, the internet's got it.

Let's look at a real-life case for perspective. Ever heard of the Nigerian Prince scam? No, it's not an off-beat fairy tale. It's a classic example of an email scam where the fraudster pretends to be a Nigerian prince who desperately needs your help transferring a massive amount of money out of the country. In return for your 'help', you're promised a chunk of that wealth. Spoiler alert: there's no prince, there's no money, and you're left with a lighter wallet.

So, how do these fraudsters make it all happen? They've got a bunch of strategies. Phishing is a big one - sending emails or texts that seem legit, like from your bank or a trusted company, tricking you into giving out personal information. Some use skimming devices on ATMs or card readers to steal your card info when you swipe. Then there are those who try old-school methods like dumpster diving to find any documents or receipts you've tossed.

I'm sure you've heard. Prevention is better cure and it applies to fraud as well. Let's take a look at the best ways to prevent fraud.

Preventing Fraud

Preventing fraud may seem like a mission for a caped superhero, but you're more powerful in this fight than you might think. You've got your own superpowers: knowledge, caution, and vigilance. Let's dive into some ways you can use them to fight the dark side of fraud.

First up, recognize the signs. It's a lot like when your Spidey senses start tingling. Unfamiliar transactions on your bank statement? Emails from your bank asking for personal info? A call from a 'government official' demanding payment for an unexpected debt? Yeah, these are all pretty fishy. And by fishy, we mean probably fraudulent.

Next, it's about defensive moves. Think of it as your personal suit of armor.

Always ensure your transactions are secure. If you're shopping online, make sure the site starts with 'https' (the 's' stands for secure). Also, be wary of public Wi-Fi when dealing with sensitive info, it can be a hacker's paradise.

Think of every email or text message you receive as a potential threat (kind of intense, I know, but it's a jungle out there). Be skeptical of any message asking for personal info, even if it looks like it's from your bank or a familiar company. When in doubt, reach out to the company directly through their official contact methods.

Always verify identities. If someone calls claiming to be from a company you deal with, don't be shy about telling them you'll call back through the company's official number. It's like checking an ID at the door - no hard feelings, just good practice.

Protective measures also include keeping your computer's antivirus software updated, using strong, unique passwords (and changing them regularly), and never sharing personal information on social media.

Now, let's talk about what you do if you spot something suspicious: report it. Like seeing something weird happening down an alley and calling the cops. It's important to alert your bank, credit card company, or the appropriate authority if you suspect fraud. Not only does it help you, but it also helps others by allowing authorities to act quickly and possibly even catch the fraudsters.

Remember, preventing fraud isn't about living in constant fear or never enjoying the convenience of online services; it's about being aware, being cautious, and keeping your guard up. With the right knowledge and habits, you're more than ready to keep fraud at bay. Next up, let's look at a specific type of fraud - identity theft.

Understanding Identity Theft

Identity theft isn't something out of a sci-fi movie. We're not talking about face-swapping villains or cloning. This kind of theft is all about your personal information - it's when someone takes your private data and uses it without your permission. Now let's break this down, shall we?

There are different ways someone can steal your identity. Financial identity theft, the most common type, involves someone using your information to take money from your bank account, open credit cards in your name, or get a loan.

Then there's medical identity theft, where someone uses your info to get medical services. There's also criminal identity theft, where someone gives your name to the police when they get arrested (talk about throwing you under the bus). And that's just scratching the surface.

For a real-world example, let's talk about Jenna. Jenna was a university student who got a call one day from a credit card company saying she was overdue on payments for a card she never applied for. After investigating, she discovered someone had opened multiple credit cards in her name and racked up tons of debt. That's a classic case of financial identity theft.

Now, what happens after identity theft? Well, it's a bit of a mess. Just ask Jenna. She spent months trying to clear her name with the credit card companies, dealing with collectors, and trying to correct her credit score. All the while, she was constantly worried about what else the thief could do with her stolen information. It was stressful and time-consuming, to say the least.

But it's not just about the immediate fallout. The effects of identity theft can linger like a bad taste in your mouth. It can damage your credit score, making it harder to get loans or credit cards in the future. It can even affect your job prospects, as some employers check credit history as part of their hiring process.

Understanding identity theft is like getting to know your enemy - once you know what you're up against, you can prepare and protect yourself better. Next, we're going to look at how you can do exactly that. It's not about turning into a paranoid hermit, but about being smart and cautious.

Preventing Identity Theft

Now that we understand the beast that is identity theft, let's talk defense. You don't need a suit of armor or a magical shield (although that would be cool), but you do need some savvy strategies to keep your personal information safe.

The first line of defense is pretty straightforward - protect your personal info like it's the secret recipe to your grandma's world-famous chocolate chip cookies. This means not giving out your Social Security number unless absolutely necessary, not carrying your passport around town (yes, some people do that), and shredding important documents before tossing them.

But wait, it's the 21st century and we're living in the digital age. Protecting your physical documents isn't enough. You've got to secure your digital info too. This involves having strong, unique passwords for all your accounts. Think less "password123" and more "9Y&$#aKd!CZ3".

But why stop there? Enter two-factor authentication (or 2FA if you want to sound tech-savvy). This is like having a secret handshake with your online accounts. Even if someone cracks your password, they'll still need that second bit of info only you have (like a code sent to your phone) to get in.

Now, I get it. You're busy. You've got school, maybe a job, friends, hobbies...

the list goes on. But amidst all this, it's crucial to keep an eye on your financial activities. This means regularly checking your bank statements and credit reports for any fishy activities. It's like the neighborhood watch but for your money. If you spot anything out of place, report it right away.

Think of it this way – the time and effort you put into preventing identity theft now is a drop in the ocean compared to dealing with it once it happens. It's like studying for a test in advance instead of cramming the night before. The former is a lot less stressful and way more effective.

So, take these tips and use them. Secure your info, monitor your accounts, and be smart about who gets your details. After all, your identity is unique to you, and it's worth protecting. The world doesn't need another you, it needs the one and only you. Stay safe out there!

What to Do If You're a Victim

Imagine for a second, you're playing an intense game of dodgeball. Out of nowhere, you get hit by a ball. Ouch. The game isn't over. You dust yourself off and keep playing. Similarly, when it comes to identity theft or fraud, getting hit is tough, but it's not game over. So, if you find yourself in this tricky spot, here's the game plan.

If you suspect that you're a victim, it's like the first rumblings of a storm. It's best not to ignore it and hope it goes away. The first step is to accept that this is happening and start acting quickly. Much like pulling off a band-aid, it's best to do it fast. Report it to your bank or credit card company. They've seen this rodeo before and can help block your cards, open new accounts, and even walk you through the next steps.

Don't stop there, though. Remember those credit reports we talked about in

Chapter 11? It's time to contact those guys, the credit bureaus. Explain the situation, and ask them to put a fraud alert on your credit report. This tells any company checking your credit to verify your identity before issuing new credit in your name. Talk about a powerful shield!

You know how in movies when something bad happens, they call the police? Well, this is no different. Reach out to your local law enforcement and file a report. They might not catch the bad guys right away, but it's a critical step in making your case.

Now comes the part where you pick up the pieces and start to rebuild. It's like cleaning up after that massive end-of-semester party you threw. It's messy, but with some work, you can get things back in order. Contact all companies where you know fraud occurred and dispute any fraudulent charges. You might need to close existing accounts or open new ones. It's a hassle, yes, but it's part of the clean-up process.

Getting through identity theft or fraud is a journey, not a sprint. It might feel like you're climbing a mountain, but remember, every step, no matter how small, brings you closer to the top. Stay persistent, and don't be afraid to ask for help.

We've covered a lot, but if there's one thing you should take away, it's this - dealing with identity theft or fraud is tough, but it's not impossible. Like acing a challenging class or nailing a complicated guitar riff, with effort, patience, and a little help, you can get through it. It's your game to win, so gear up, step up, and take charge.

Remember, this isn't a 'read once and forget' type of thing. Keeping our guard up and being vigilant is an ongoing process, just like working out or eating healthy. Staying educated about these topics is like regular exercise for your financial health. You wouldn't want to lose those gains, right?

So, what's next on our quest? Well, as your tour guide through this digital wilderness, I challenge you to take what you've learned and put it into action. Review the security measures you have in place. Do they look like a strong fortress, or are there gaps a sneaky goblin could slip through?

Take some time to think about how you could improve. Maybe it's time to update those old passwords, or perhaps it's worth getting a more secure wallet for your credit cards. Every little change contributes to a safer future for you.

In the end, it's your life, and you're the hero of your own story. We've equipped you with some powerful knowledge - it's up to you to use it. Keep learning, stay vigilant, and above all, take control. You've got this!

We've journeyed through the lands of contracts, dodged the pitfalls of insurance, and fortified our defenses against financial fraudsters. Now, it's time to check if you're ready to wield these new skills in the real world.

So, let's dive into our Quiz Arena! Consider it a friendly sparring match to test your new know-how. Remember, the goal isn't just to get all the answers right, but to reflect on what you've learned and understand where you might need to revisit. So buckle up, put on your thinking cap, and let's see how you do in our quick-fire round of financial trivia.

Ready, Set, Recall

Welcome to the final challenge of this journey! Time to test your knowledge about contracts, insurance, and the ins and outs of preventing fraud and identity theft. Remember, don't stress over it; this quiz is designed as a tool to help reinforce your learning. Give it a go, and if you feel unsure about any answers, you can always revisit the chapters. Don't forget, the answer key can be found in the resources section at the back of the book.

1. What is a contract?
   a) An agreement between two parties.
   b) A legal document that outlines the duties and obligations of each party.
   c) A form of insurance.
   d) Both a and b.

2. What is the primary purpose of insurance?
   a) To protect against potential financial losses.
   b) To ensure you never lose money.
   c) To increase your wealth.
   d) None of the above.

3. What is a premium in terms of insurance?
   a) The maximum amount the insurance company will pay.
   b) The amount you pay monthly or annually to maintain your insurance

coverage.

    c) The deductible you must pay before your insurance coverage starts.

    d) The amount you receive from the insurance company when a claim is made.

4. What is fraud?

    a) A method of identity theft.

    b) A dishonest act or statement made with the intent to deceive.

    c) A type of insurance policy.

    d) A type of contract.

5. What are some common methods used in identity theft?

    a) Phishing emails.

    b) Data breaches.

    c) Stolen mail or wallets.

    d) All of the above.

6. How can you protect yourself from fraud?

    a) By never sharing personal information.

    b) By regularly monitoring your bank and credit card statements.

    c) By using strong, unique passwords.

    d) All of the above.

7. What should you do if you become a victim of identity theft?

    a) Report it to the police.

    b) Notify your bank and credit card companies.

    c) Place a fraud alert on your credit reports.

    d) All of the above.

8. What is a deductible in an insurance policy?

    a) The amount you must pay before the insurance company will cover the rest.

    b) The amount you pay for the insurance policy.

c) The amount you must pay after the insurance company covers their part.

d) The total amount the insurance company will pay in case of a loss.

9. Why is it essential to read contracts thoroughly before signing?

a) To understand your rights and obligations.

b) To identify any potential pitfalls or unfavorable terms.

c) Because once signed, it's legally binding.

d) All of the above.

10. What is the relationship between contracts and insurance?

a) Insurance policies are contracts between the insurer and the insured.

b) Both are forms of financial risk management.

c) Both can protect against potential financial losses.

d) All of the above.

VIII

Part 8 - Beyond Personal Finance

Chapter 20 - Charitable Giving and Social Responsibility

W e're diving into a topic that's super essential but doesn't often grab the spotlight in our daily money talk - the universe of giving back and doing some serious good. Sounds heavy-duty, right? Well, it is. But hang tight - once you get a grip on it, you'll realize it's actually pretty epic.

At the heart of giving back, there's the beautiful act of sharing. But hey, it's not just about tossing some coins to a charity (although that's part of it). It's about wrapping your head around an attitude of kindness, where you're ready to part with a piece of your pie - your cash, your free hours, even your mad skills - to light up someone's world. And here's the best part - you don't need to be rolling in dough to shake things up. Even the smallest good deeds can rock someone's world.

Now, let's chew over this thing that's been buzzing around called social responsibility. It's a hot topic lately, and it's pretty much the twin of giving back. It's all about realizing that we're part of this crazy, interconnected web and our actions can ripple out and touch others. So, it's about being switched on and giving a hoot about our fellow earthlings and the big, beautiful world we share.

But why the heck should all of this matter to you? Well, here's the clincher.

Giving back is a colossal cog in the wheel that powers the organizations tirelessly grinding to make our world more awesome. Think about the local food drives, the eco-warriors battling climate change, and those brainy folks trying to crack the code to cure diseases - they all run on the generosity of people just like us.

In a nutshell, giving back and social responsibility are all about doing your bit to spruce up our world. It's about linking arms with others in this global mission and playing your part.

Why Sharing is Seriously Cool: All the Good Vibes for You and the World

So, let's chat about this whole idea of giving. Why should you even bother? What's in it for you and what's the big deal for everyone else? Hold on to your hats, 'cause the perks of giving are more mind-blowing than you'd guess.

Let's kick this off with the personal wins. At first glance, giving might look like you're handing over something valuable, right? Here's the surprise twist, though—studies show that folks who give often wind up feeling way happier and more content with their lives. How come? Well, when you give, your brain gets this super cool message that you have plenty to go around, which makes you feel safe and satisfied. Plus, there's the whole heart-melting, grin-making feeling of knowing you've lit up someone else's day. So, it's a double-whammy of feel-good vibes!

But wait, there's more. Let's dish about the ripple effect your giving can create. Picture this—you're tossing a stone into a lake. That initial splash may seem tiny, but those ripples? They can spread far and wide. When you give, you're creating ripples of awesomeness across your neighborhood, city, or even the entire globe. Maybe you're donating to a local food bank, which can help folks in your community keep their cupboards stocked. Or you're spending time tutoring in an after-school program, helping kids smash their academic goals. Every act of giving is a stone that starts ripples of change.

But hey, let's ground this in reality. Ever heard of Mr. Beast (you know, real name Jimmy Donaldson)? He's a mega-popular YouTuber who's famous for his epic generosity. With a subscriber count over 150 million, he's made headlines for crazy stuff like giving away a whole island or donating tons of cash to total strangers. And while not all of us can be Mr. Beast, his story is a reminder that we can all stir up big waves of change with a giving heart.

So, the bottom line? Giving isn't just about the cash you shell out or the time you devote to volunteering. It's about the positive energy that surges from your kind acts and sweeps across the world. It's about the warm and fuzzy feelings that bubble up inside you and the difference you make in the lives of others. So even though it might look like you're parting with something, what you gain in return is pretty epic.

Picking Your Passion: Finding Charities and Causes You Dig

Alright, you're feeling the buzz around giving. But where do you even start? With so many charities and causes out there, how do you pick the right ones? Let's dive in and explore that.

What's Your Jam? Tuning into Your Values and Passions

The best place to start? Inside your own heart. Yeah, seriously. Pause for a sec and think about the stuff that matters to you most. What issues fire you up? What tugs at your heartstrings? Maybe you're all about protecting the environment or you have a soft spot for animals. Perhaps you're super passionate about education, fighting poverty, or supporting mental health.

Whatever it is, get clear on what resonates with you, 'cause that's going to be your guiding light in this giving journey.

Doing Your Homework on Charities and Non-Profits

Next up, it's time to put on your detective hat. Once you've got a shortlist of issues that matter to you, start scoping out the charities and non-profits working in those areas. The thing is, you want to make sure your donations are going to have the biggest impact, right? So, it's crucial to dig into stuff like how they use their funds, their track record of success, and what experts and donors are saying about them. Sites like Charity Navigator and GuideStar can be super handy for this, offering ratings and detailed info to help you make an informed decision.

Cash, Caring, and Cutbacks: Unraveling the Tax Perks of Giving

So, you're thinking about making a difference and donating some cash? Well, we have some more good news for you. The taxman actually wants to give you a pat on the back for your generosity. Let's dive into this whole charitable giving tax situation. It's kinda like getting a gold star for doing good.

Can We Deduct? The Lowdown on Tax Deductions for Donations

So here's the deal: when you give money to certain charities, you can write those donations off on your taxes. And that means you get to pay Uncle Sam a little less at tax time. Yep, it's like a little thank-you note from the government for being a kind human. But remember, keep track of those donations - a receipt or even a 'thanks-for-your-donation' email can help you out, come tax time.

Setting the Rules: What Actually Counts as a Charitable Contribution?

But hold on, before you start imagining all the tax breaks you'll be getting, let's clarify what counts as a 'charitable contribution.' Simply put, you can't just give money to anyone or anything and expect a tax break. It's gotta be a legit non-profit organization. That means buying lemonade from your little cousin's lemonade stand or tossing a few bucks into a street performer's guitar case, while super kind, won't earn you any tax perks. Also, just so you know, you can only deduct up to a certain percentage of your income (usually it hovers around 50-60%).

So, here's the bottom line: Giving back doesn't just make you feel awesome—it can also help your wallet out a bit. By getting the hang of these tax rules, you can make your act of kindness go even further. It's a win for you, a win for the charity, and most importantly, a win for the cause you're supporting. Can't argue with that!

Getting the Giving Groove On: How to Make Charitable Donations a Regular Part of Your Life

So you're keen to become a regular do-gooder? Let's dive into how you can incorporate this into your everyday life.

What's In Your Wallet: Setting a Giving Budget

First things first, how much do you donate? It's a pretty personal decision and depends on your financial situation and comfort level. Some folks aim for a "tithing" model, which means handing over 10% of their income. But it's all up to you. Maybe for you, it's more like 3%, 7%, or even 15%. The key point here? You're doing something awesome, no matter the amount.

Once in a Blue Moon or Every Full Moon: Regular Donations or One-Time Giving

Alright, next up: how often should you be parting with your cash? Some people prefer to donate a larger amount once a year, whereas others like to break it up across the year. Both options have their pros. Regular donations can provide a charity with a steady income stream. However, one-time donations can be particularly helpful, especially during urgent appeals.

Outside the Donation Box: Creative Giving Ideas

Now, if you think charitable giving means only money, think again. There's a whole universe of options out there. Ever thought of joining a charity walk or organizing a fundraiser for your birthday? These are amazing ways to rally your friends and community for your cause. There's also this thing called "planned giving" where you can leave a legacy by including a charity in your will.

Turning charitable giving into a regular thing is more than just making a positive change in the world (although that's a huge plus). It's about growing into someone who actively looks out for others and makes a difference. And that, dear reader, is a journey worth embarking on. So get out there, make your giving plan, and revel in the good vibes that come from doing good.

Looking Into the Future: Where's Charitable Giving Heading?

So you're now up to speed with the whole concept of giving, its benefits and how you can get involved. But let's take a sneak peek into the future. How's the world of giving changing and what can we expect going forward?

Making Donations Click: The Digital and Crowdfunding Boom

Remember the times when you had to sign checks or hand over cash to donate? Well, times have changed. Now, all you need is your device – laptop, phone, tablet, you name it – and voila, you're in the world of giving. Whether you're clicking on a donate button or supporting a cause through crowdfunding, giving has become a piece of cake.

Speaking of crowdfunding, it's pretty much the superstar of the giving world right now. Thanks to platforms like GoFundMe, Kickstarter, and others, individuals and organizations can connect directly to us, telling their stories and asking for our support. It's all about lots of small donations adding up to make a big difference.

Charities Meet Hashtags: Social Media Stepping Up

If you're into Instagram, Twitter, TikTok, or pretty much any social media, you've probably seen posts about various charities. From awareness campaigns to online fundraisers, social media is buzzing with charitable causes. It's not only about donating but also about sharing, spreading the word, and getting people engaged with causes that matter. Remember when everyone was dumping buckets of ice water over their heads for ALS research? Yeah, that's the power of social media!

Gazing into the Crystal Ball: What's Coming in Charitable Giving?

So, what does the future hold for giving? Well, there are some pretty exciting trends brewing. Technology is playing a massive role, with things like virtual reality and artificial intelligence starting to show up in the charity scene. Imagine experiencing what a charity does through a VR headset! Plus, there's a growing emphasis on showing donors how their contributions are making a real difference.

So, the future of giving is already here, and it's looking exciting and packed with opportunities. Whether you're giving a few bucks via a crowdfunding site or launching a viral charity challenge on your social media, remember that every little bit counts.

The Final Stop: You're Part of This Huge Change

From understanding why it's a big deal to figuring out how you can be part of it. We've seen how giving shapes us and the world we live in, and most importantly, how it reminds us that we can make things happen.

Creating a habit of giving isn't a one-and-done deal. It's a long-term commitment, and the good news is, you have a lifetime to perfect it. Start small, find your groove, and keep adding to it. Maybe it's setting aside some money each month to donate, spending a few hours volunteering, or even just spreading the word about a cause close to your heart. The point is, keep going. The journey starts right here, right now.

Before we wrap up, here's a final thought to keep in mind. Each time you give, you're making an impact. Yup, every single act counts. The effects might not always be immediate, but trust us, they're there. Your donation could be the reason a family gets to enjoy a decent meal. The hours you volunteer could help an organization do more. Your voice could draw attention to an important cause.

As you continue this journey, remember that you've got the power to make a difference. You can help shape the world into a better place. Keep on giving!

Ready, Set, Recall

You've absorbed an ocean of financial knowledge throughout this journey. From understanding money to exploring the world of investing, and now you've tackled topics beyond personal finance. It's time to see how well you remember what you've learned. Remember, it's okay to get some wrong. Learning is a journey, not a race. The answers are found in the resources chapter at the back, so you can check your work when you're done.

1. Why is charitable giving beneficial?
    a) It helps support causes you care about.
    b) It can provide tax benefits.
    c) It can promote a sense of social responsibility.
    d) All of the above

2. What should you consider when choosing a charity?
    a) The cause they support.
    b) How they use their funds.
    c) Their credibility and reputation.
    d) All of the above

3. What is one potential benefit of donating to charity on your taxes?
    a) You might get a thank-you note.
    b) It might be tax-deductible.

c) You can claim it as income.

d) It raises your tax bracket.

Before We Say Goodbye!

W e trust that "The Essential Money Skills Handbook for Teens" has provided you with invaluable insights to navigate your financial journey. Your time and commitment to deepening your understanding of money matters are admirable, and we'd be delighted if you could spare just a minute to share your thoughts with us.

Your feedback is not just significant to us but also to other teens, parents, and educators who are exploring the world of financial literacy. By leaving a review, you can guide others towards making informed financial decisions and empower them to gain control over their money matters.

We appreciate your contribution in spreading the word about the book and its impact. Remember, you have the ability to influence and encourage others on their path to mastering their finances. Together, let's equip the next generation with the financial skills and knowledge they need to thrive. Your one minute can make a world of difference, so we thank you for your time and your support.

Customer reviews

★★★★½ 4.7 out of 5

221 global ratings

5 star	▓▓▓▓▓▓▓░░	76%
4 star	▓▓░░░░░░░	20%
3 star	▓░░░░░░░░	3%
2 star	░░░░░░░░░	1%
1 star	░░░░░░░░░	1%

⌄ How customer reviews and ratings work

Review this product

Share your thoughts with other customers

Write a customer review

Scan this QR code to leave a quick 1-minute review

Your feedback is incredibly valuable, not only for us but also for other parents and educators seeking guidance on financial literacy for teens. By sharing your thoughts, you'll contribute to the growth and improvement of RaiseYouthRight. Our hope is that with the information we share, we can make the next generation healthier, wealthier, and happier than ours!

We appreciate your support and look forward to diving into Part 2, where we'll explore practical ways to apply these valuable career planning tools.

Conclusion

Y ou've made it to the finish line—almost. The real journey's just about to kick off, and you're in the driver's seat. As you cruise down the road of finance, remember this: money's not just about dollars and cents, it's about mindset. Think of money as a tool that helps you chase your dreams, not just something you 'need to survive.' When you start seeing money as an opportunity and not just an obligation, you'll find the game gets way more exciting.

So, what have we learned? We've covered the basics from budgeting and investing to future money trends. We've talked about making smart choices, not being scared of the financial world, and remembering that it's okay to ask for help. We've delved into the exciting and sometimes mind-boggling world of cryptocurrency and fintech. But the most important thing we've discovered? You're in control. Your financial future is in your hands, and with the right knowledge and attitude, you've got this.

Before we say goodbye, let's talk about a few more tools that could help you on your financial journey. There are tons of apps and platforms out there designed to help you manage your money. From budgeting apps like Mint and You Need a Budget (YNAB), to expense trackers like Expensify, these tools can be super handy.

Just remember, like everything else in finance, the best tool is the one that works for you. So take your time, explore your options, and find your perfect match.

And with that, we're at the end. But remember, this isn't really 'the end.' It's the beginning of your financial journey. So go forth, stay curious, and remember: you've got this. You're more prepared than you think, and the world of finance is ready for you to make your mark. So let's go conquer the world—one budget at a time.

Resources and Bibliography

Resources and Bibliography

Quiz Answer Keys

Part 1

1. b) Money is a universal medium of exchange

2. b) The trust that people place in it

3. b) Because of inflation

4. b) The cost of goods and services decreases

5. a) By changing interest rates

6. b) Virtual currency that exists only in the digital world

7. c) Blockchain technology

8. c) Bitcoin

9. c) It depends on the laws of the country you are in

10. b) For mobile payments

Part 2

1. c) Interest from loans

2. a) Checking accounts are for spending, savings accounts are for saving

3. b) A type of savings account that usually requires a higher balance but earns more interest

4. b) Special bank accounts that lock your money for a certain period in exchange for higher interest rates

5. c) Salary from a job

6. a) Income you earn while sleeping or not actively working

7. c) Earnings from a blog or YouTube channel that you monetize

8. a) Different careers have different average income levels

9. b) They influence the amount of money you earn or pay in interest

10. a) Technology has opened up new opportunities to earn income, such as blogging or vlogging

11. c) The money you owe to the government based on your income.

12. b) A detailed explanation of what your pay consists of, including gross pay, net pay, and any deductions.

13. b) To explain complex tax laws and help with filing tax returns.

14. a) A W-2 form.

15. a) You might face penalties or interest charges from the IRS.

16. c) Being mindful of how your financial decisions affect society.

17. b) To ensure you're being paid accurately and understand deductions.

Part 3

1. c) To help you manage your money and plan for the future

2. b) A 'need' is something you can't live without, a 'want' is something you would like to have

3. b) Because of compound interest

4. a) Money set aside for unexpected expenses

5. c) Saving contributes to your financial plan and helps you reach your financial goals

6. b) It helps you plan and prioritize your savings

7. b) The desire to experience pleasure or fulfillment without delay or

deferment

8. c) Someone who makes thoughtful decisions about their spending

9. b) Ignoring small expenses

10. b) Because it allows your money to grow exponentially over time

Part 4

1. c) A credit card lets you borrow money, a debit card does not

2. c) Birthday Present

3. c) Making sure you pay your debts on time and effectively reducing what you owe over time

4. a) A rating that determines your trustworthiness as a borrower

5. d) All of the above

6. c) Paying your bills on time, keeping your balance low, and being cautious about opening new credit cards

7. b) Yes, your credit score can impact your ability to get a loan or credit card and the interest rate you're offered

8. b) Take steps to improve it, like paying bills on time, reducing debt, and avoiding new debt

9. b) The terms and conditions outline important details like interest rates,

penalties, and fees

10. b) Request a report from a credit bureau or use a reputable online service

Part 5

1. c) Funds you borrow to pay for higher education

2. b) Grants are based on financial need, scholarships on merit

3. d) Consider your future earning potential, living expenses, and tuition costs

4. a) To maximize compound interest

5. c) Certificate of Deposit (CD)

6. b) It's a program where workers earn credits for retirement benefits

7. d) Excessive savings

8. c) A new car depreciates faster but comes with a warranty, a used car costs less upfront but may have higher maintenance costs

9. d) All of the above

10. a) Your beliefs and attitudes about money

11. d) All of the above

12. a) It can prevent you from making good financial decisions

13. a) Practicing gratitude

14. d) All of the above

15. b) Your savings strategy and timeline

16. b) To alleviate stress and bring more joy into your life

17. b) They supplement Social Security and personal savings, providing additional income during retirement

Part 6

1. b) A piece of ownership in a company

2. b) Spread your investments across various types of assets

3. c) The idea that money available now is worth more than the same amount in the future because of its potential earning capacity

4. b) A loan made to a company or government

5. b) A collection of investments, such as stocks or bonds

6. a) It can help you avoid making impulsive decisions based on short-term market fluctuations

7. c) It takes advantage of dollar-cost averaging, which can lower the average cost per share of an investment

8. d) Where the company's cash is coming from and where it's being used

9. a) The idea that investments with higher risk tend to offer higher potential returns

10. b) The process of buying, owning, managing, renting, or selling real estate for profit

Part 7

1.d) Both b and c.

2. c) To increase your wealth

3. b) The amount you pay monthly or annually to keep your insurance coverage.

4. b) It's always a type of identity theft.

5. b) Breaking into your home to steal personal documents.

6. b) Using the same password for all your accounts.

7. a) Confront the person you suspect.

8.a) The amount you must pay before the insurance company will cover the rest.

9.d) All of the above.

10.d) Insurance policies are contracts that detail the terms of coverage.

Part 8

1. d) All of the above.

2. d) All of the above.

3. b) It might be tax-deductible.

Resources and Helpful Links

Websites/Blogs:

Investopedia's "Understanding Currency" - https://www.investopedia.com/terms/c/currency.asp

Bitcoin.org: Getting Started with Bitcoin - https://bitcoin.org/en/getting-started

Coindesk's Cryptocurrency for Beginners - https://www.coindesk.com/learn/cryptocurrency

Investopedia: Active vs. Passive Income https://www.investopedia.com/financial-edge/0810/active-vs.-passive-income.aspx

The Balance: Careers https://www.thebalancecareers.com/

Smart Passive Income https://www.smartpassiveincome.com/

NerdWallet: Budgeting 101 https://www.nerdwallet.com/

The Balance: Frugal Living https://www.thebalance.com/frugal-living-4074014

The Balance: Understanding Different Types of Debt https://www.thebalance.com/types-of-debt-2385982

Credit.com: Beginner's Guide to Managing Debt https://www.credit.com/debt/five-step-checklist-for-managing-debt/

Experian: What is a Good Credit Score? https://www.experian.com/blogs/ask-experian/credit-education/score-basics/what-is-a-good-credit-score/

Credit Karma: Understanding Credit https://www.creditkarma.com/advice/i/how-to-build-credit-from-scratch

Federal Student Aid https://studentaid.gov/

Scholarships.com https://www.scholarships.com/

Investopedia: Retiremen https://www.investopedia.com/retirement/

The Balance: Retirement Planning (https://www.thebalance.com/retirement-planning-4074004

Nerdwallet: Home Buying https://www.nerdwallet.com/mortgages/home-buying

Ramit Sethi's I Will Teach You To Be Rich Blog https://www.iwillteachyoutoberich.com/blog/

Investor.gov https://www.investor.gov/

The College Investor https://thecollegeinvestor.com

Morningstar https://www.morningstar.com/

Investopedia's Simulator https://www.investopedia.com/simulator/

Charity Navigator https://www.charitynavigator.org/

GuideStar https://www.guidestar.org/

Apps

Coinbase https://www.coinbase.com/

Chime https://www.chime.com/

Upwork https://www.upwork.com/

Acorns https://www.acorns.com/

Mint https://www.mint.com/

PocketGuard https://www.pocketguard.com/

Honey https://www.joinhoney.com/

CamelCamelCamel https://camelcamelcamel.com/

Digit https://digit.co/

You Need a Budget (YNAB) https://www.youneedabudget.com/

Scholly https://myscholly.com/

Navient https://navient.com/

Stash https://www.stash.com/

AutoGravity https://www.autogravity.com/

Zillow https://www.zillow.com/

ThinkUp https://thinkup.me/

Robinhood https://robinhood.com/us/en/

Seeking Alpha https://seekingalpha.com/

Charity Miles https://charitymiles.org/

Givz https://givz.com/

Books

"The History of Money" by Jack Weatherford

"Rich Dad Poor Dad for Teens" by Robert Kiyosaki

"Bitcoin and Cryptocurrency Technologies: A Comprehensive Introduction" by Arvind Narayanan et al.

"Your Money or Your Life" by Vicki Robin & Joe Dominguez

"The Total Money Makeover" by Dave Ramsey

"The Richest Man in Babylon" by George S. Clason

"The Automatic Millionaire" by David Bach

"Your Score: An Insider's Secrets to Understanding, Controlling, and Protecting Your Credit Score" by Anthony Davenport

"Debt-Free Degree: The Step-by-Step Guide to Getting Your Kid Through College Without Student Loans" by Anthony ONeal

"The Automatic Millionaire: A Powerful One-Step Plan to Live and Finish Rich" by David Bach

"You Are a Badass at Making Money: Master the Mindset of Wealth" by Jen Sincero

"The Little Book of Common Sense Investing" by John C. Bogle

"A Random Walk Down Wall Street" by Burton G. Malkiel

Courses

Coursera: Bitcoin and Cryptocurrency Technologies https://www.coursera.or g/learn/cryptocurrency

Khan Academy: Saving and Budgeting https://www.khanacademy.org/colleg e-careers-more/personal-finance/pf-saving-and-budgeting

Khan Academy: Understanding and Managing Credit https://www.khanacad emy.org/college-careers-more/personal-finance/personal-finance-credit-cards-credit-reports/a/understanding-and-managing-credit

Khan Academy's Macroeconomics Course – https://www.khanacademy.org/ economics-finance-domain/macroeconomics

Investing 101: Stock Market Course for Beginners https://www.skillshare.com /classes/Investing-101-Stock-Market-Course-for-Beginners/2128851016

Videos/Podcasts:

Planet Money https://www.npr.org/sections/money/127413729/planet-mon ey/

TED Talk: How the blockchain is changing money and business https://www.t ed.com/talks/don_tapscott_how_the_blockchain_is_changing_money_ and_business

Unchained Podcast https://unchainedpodcast.com/

GaryVee Podcast https://www.garyvaynerchuk.com/podcast/

TED Talks: How to get better at the things you care about https://www.ted .com/talks/eduardo_briceno_how_to_get_better_at_the_things_you_ care_about

The Dave Ramsey Show https://www.daveramsey.com/show

YouTube: Budget With Me https://www.youtube.com/results?search_query =budget+with+me

The Minimalists Podcast https://www.theminimalists.com/podcast/

YouTube: The Financial Diet https://www.youtube.com/c/TheFinancialDiet

BiggerPockets Money Podcast https://www.biggerpockets.com/moneyshow

YouTube: Graham Stephan https://www.youtube.com/c/GrahamStephan

InvestED Podcast https://www.ruleoneinvesting.com/podcast/

The Minority Mindset on YouTube https://www.youtube.com/channel/UCT3 EznhW_CNFcfOlyDNTLLw

About the Author

Scarlett Rivers is a passionate writer and valued member of RaiseYouthRight, a publishing company dedicated to equipping children, teens, and young adults with essential life skills. With her captivating storytelling and insightful approach, Scarlett has become a trusted voice in the realm of personal development and growth for the younger generation.

From cultivating emotional intelligence and effective communication skills to embracing resilience and fostering a positive mindset, Scarlett's works offer practical tools and guidance to navigate the challenges of the modern world.

Scarlett's writing style effortlessly combines relatability with wisdom, as she draws from her own experiences and struggles during her formative years. As a young adult who overcame adversity and discovered her own path to self-fulfillment, Scarlett understands the unique hurdles faced by her readers and empathizes with their journeys.

Motivated by a deep desire to make a positive impact, Scarlett joined RaiseYouthRight to amplify her reach and inspire young minds on a global scale. By empowering teenagers and young adults with the knowledge and skills they don't typically learn in school, Scarlett aims to foster personal growth, resilience, and confidence in her readers.

With each book she writes, Scarlett aspires to ignite a sense of curiosity, self-reflection, and empowerment within her audience. By embracing her transformative words, young readers can embark on a lifelong journey of self-discovery, building a strong foundation for a fulfilling and successful future.

Through her work at RaiseYouthRight, Scarlett Rivers is committed to nurturing the next generation, one page at a time, and helping them unlock their true potential.

You can connect with me on:
- ⊕ https://raiseyouthright.com
- 🐦 https://twitter.com/raiseyouthright
- 📘 https://www.facebook.com/raiseyouthright

Also by RaiseYouthRight

Richard Meadows is the founder of RaiseYouthRight, a publishing company dedicated to sharing practical wisdom that empowers the next generation to lead healthier, wealthier, and happier lives. As a bestselling author and mentor to teens, Richard combines his personal experience as a teenager with his passion for guiding young people.

His books, including the highly acclaimed "The Essential Social Skills Handbook for Teens," tackle crucial topics such as social anxiety, confidence building, stress management, and academic and mindset guidance. Richard's unique approach is tailored to the specific needs of teenagers and young adults, providing clear and relatable guidance they can implement in their daily lives.

Having experienced his own struggles with self-esteem, confidence, and social anxiety during his youth, Richard understands firsthand the challenges faced by teenagers today. He embarked on a personal journey of self-discovery, utilizing the strategies he learned through reading and applying them to heal and grow.

Recognizing that not all young people have access to the support they need, Richard is driven to make a difference through his writing. His ultimate goal is to ensure that practical guidance and resources are readily available to every teenager seeking to overcome their obstacles and thrive in their journey toward adulthood. With RaiseYouthRight, Richard is on a mission to inspire and empower the next generation to reach their full potential.

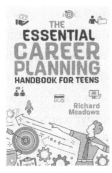

The Essential Career Planning Handbook for Teens

Discover the ultimate career planning guide designed specifically for teens in the modern era. In "The Essential Career Planning Handbook for Teens," unlock the keys to crafting a path towards a fulfilling and successful future. Packed with expert guidance, actionable strategies, and empowering advice, this book equips both teens and parents with the tools they need to navigate the complex world of career choices and opportunities. From unleashing their unique strengths to mastering the art of networking, teens will gain invaluable insights to propel their career journey forward. Don't leave their future to chance—grab your copy today and embark on an adventure that will shape their path for years to come. The journey to a thriving career starts now!

The Essential Stress Management Handbook for Teens

Discover the ultimate stress management guide designed specifically for teens in the post-pandemic era. In "The Essential Stress Management Handbook for Teens," you'll unlock the keys to conquering stress and empowering your teens to thrive. With practical strategies, proven techniques, and personalized advice, this book equips both teens and parents with the tools they need to navigate the pressures of school, digital overload, and social challenges. From agile stress-relief techniques to habit-forming exercises, you'll learn how to transform stress-busting hacks into natural instincts that empower your teens to tackle stress head-on. Don't let stress hinder your teens' happiness and success—grab your copy today and embark on a journey toward a stress-free and fulfilling life.

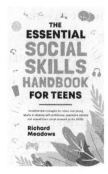

The Essential Social Skills Handbook for Teens

Unlock your teen's full potential with "The Essential Social Skills Handbook for Teens." If your teen struggles with anxiety, lack of confidence, or shyness, this book is the transformative solution you've been searching for. Written by an author who has personally overcome these challenges, this handbook offers practical techniques and valuable insights to boost your teen's confidence in just 30 days. Say goodbye to social anxieties and hello to a new level of self-assurance. From effective communication strategies to mastering social interactions, this book covers it all. With proven methods and bonus templates, your teen will develop the skills needed to thrive in social situations, set goals, and unleash their true potential. Don't let your teen miss out on the opportunity to become the socially confident individual they deserve to be.

Made in United States
North Haven, CT
25 September 2023

41970538R10148